Mary Engelbreit's
Sweet Treats
Dessert Cookbook

Mary Engelbreit's
Sweet Treats
Dessert Cookbook

ILLUSTRATED BY MARY ENGELBREIT

Photographs by Alison Miksch

**Andrews McMeel
Publishing**

Kansas City

www.andrewsmcmeel.com
www.maryengelbreit.com

 is a registered trademark of Mary Engelbreit Enterprises, Inc.

Library of Congress Cataloging-in-Publication Data

Engelbreit, Mary.
    Mary Engelbreit's sweet treats : dessert cookbook / illustrated
by Mary Engelbreit ; photographs by Alison Miksch.
      p. cm.
    Includes index.
    ISBN 0-7407-0319-6 (hc.)
    1. Desserts. I. Title.
    TX773 .E54 1999
    641.8'6—dc21   99-32149
                                            CIP

First U.S. Edition
00 01 02 10 9 8 7 6 5 4 3 2

Recipe developers: Melissa Clark & Judith Sutton
Editor: Sarah Stewart
Designer: Alexandra Maldonado
Photographer: Alison Miksch

Printed in Great Britain by
Butler & Tanner Ltd., Frome and London

Produced by Smallwood & Stewart, Inc., New York City

ATTENTION: SCHOOLS AND BUSINESSES
Andrews McMeel books are available at quantity discounts with bulk purchase for educational, business, or sales promotional use.
For information, please write to: Special Sales Department, Andrews McMeel Publishing, 4520 Main Street, Kansas City, Missouri 64111.

table of *contents*

introduction

ALMOST EVERYONE HAS A WEAKNESS FOR DESSERTS. They are the sweet treats that are packed in school lunch boxes, the luscious fruit pie whose fragrance fills the kitchen, the triumphant cake that is the centerpiece of a birthday party or the grand finale to a special meal.

I suppose this passion for sweets begins early, with our first chores in the kitchen; shaping dough or cleaning out the mixing bowls with a wooden spoon. Whether or not we graduate to higher culinary efforts, the die is very often cast. We have been introduced to the magic that turns sugar, eggs and flour into crisp sweet cookies or a spectacular cake.

Of course, this culinary magic is, in truth, available to us all. And here, in the following pages, some dessert experts show how we all can produce sensational sweets for family dinners and festive occasions alike. From childhood treats to comforting classics to the glamorous stars of the dessert table, many of my favorites are included and plenty more besides. Most are surprisingly simple and quick to prepare and all are sure to work their special magic on family and friends.

Mary

Queen of the Kitchen Tips

How to Measure

Because baking is a much more exact science than cooking, precise measuring is essential. Certain ingredients even require specific measuring techniques.

● To measure dry ingredients, use "dry" measuring cups. Choose a metal or a sturdy plastic set that includes 1/4-cup, 1/3-cup, 1/2-cup, and 1-cup sizes. Some specialty kitchenware shops now offer 2/3-cup and 3/4-cup measures as well, which can be handy if you bake a lot. Dip the appropriate cup into the ingredient, such as flour, granulated sugar, or cocoa, overfilling it slightly. Do not tap the cup on the counter or pack down the ingredient. Using a sweeping motion, level off the top with a metal spatula or the straight edge of a knife. (This is sometimes referred to as the dip-and-sweep method.)

● To measure brown sugar, use a dry measuring cup. Firmly pack the sugar into the cup, pressing down on it and overfilling the cup slightly. Use a metal spatula or the straight edge of a knife to level off the top.

● If you have canned vegetable shortening rather than the newer sticks, you should also use this method to measure it.

● To measure liquid ingredients, use clear glass measuring cups with pouring spouts, available in 1-cup, 2-cup, and 4-cup sizes. (Glass cups tend to be more accurate than plastic ones.) Place the cup on a level surface, such as the kitchen counter. Fill the cup to the appropriate level, then check the measure at eye level; don't lift up the cup to read it.

● Measuring spoons, used to measure small amounts of both dry and liquid ingredients, usually come in sets of four: 1/4 teaspoon, 1/2 teaspoon, 1 teaspoon, and 1 tablespoon. Some also include a 1/2-tablespoon measure. Good-quality metal or sturdy plastic measuring spoons are the most accurate. To measure dry ingredients, such as baking powder and baking soda, dip the spoon into the ingredient, slightly overfilling it, and level off the top as for dry measuring cups. To measure liquid ingredients, such as vanilla or lemon juice, simply pour them into the spoon up to the rim.

● To measure butter, margarine, and stick shortening, use the marks printed on the wrapper in tablespoons, ounces, and fractions of a cup. Cut off the desired amount with a sharp knife.

● To measure sour cream, yogurt, and similar ingredients, use dry rather than liquid measuring cups. Spoon the ingredient into the cup, then level off the top with a metal spatula or the straight edge of a knife.

Ingredients

BAKING POWDER: Baking powder is a leavener that helps cakes and other baked goods rise. Most baking powder is "double-acting," meaning that it reacts first when it comes in contact with moisture (such as milk in a cake batter) and then when exposed to the heat of the oven. Baking powder loses its effectiveness if it's too old. To test it, combine a teaspoon or so with 1/4 cup hot water; if it bubbles, it's still good.

BAKING SODA: Baking soda is a leavener like baking powder, but reacts just once, when it's combined with liquid. For this reason, after you've added baking soda to the batter, you should get the batter into the pan and then the pan into the oven as soon as possible so that the baking soda doesn't lose its effectiveness.

BUTTER: Bakers like to use unsalted (sometimes labeled "sweet") rather than salted butter for two reasons: Unsalted tends to be fresher than salted because salt acts a preservative and can mask off-flavors. Using unsalted butter also allows greater control over the actual amount of salt in the recipe, since the only salt is what the baker adds, not the unknown amount in the butter.

COCOA POWDER: Unsweetened cocoa powder may be "Dutch-processed" (also called alkalized), or not. "Dutched" cocoa has a darker color and a deeper but more mellow chocolate flavor than nonalkalized cocoa. Although in many cases the two can be used interchangeably, some recipes taste better made with one or the other. (Don't use cocoa mixes, which have added sugar and other ingredients, for baking.)

CREAM: For recipes that call for heavy cream, you can use either "heavy" or "whipping" (sometimes labeled "heavy whipping") cream. Heavy cream is slightly richer than whipping cream.

EGGS: For the recipes in this book, use Grade A large. Buy only clean, uncracked eggs and keep them refrigerated. Egg whites whip to a greater volume if they are at room temperature, but it's easier to separate eggs when they're cold. So if a recipe calls for separating eggs or just for egg whites, separate the eggs while they are still refrigerator-cold, but allow the whites to stand at room temperature for 10 to 15 minutes before beating them.

EXTRACTS: Always use pure extracts if you can. They have a much better flavor than artificially flavored ones.

SPICES: Spices are perishable and lose both their fragrance and color over time. Store them in tightly sealed containers in a cool, dry place (not on top of the stove, even though that's temptingly convenient) and check them before using: A sniff or two will tell you whether they're still fresh. If they're not aromatic, replace them. Generally, ground spices have a shelf life of about six months.

ZEST: Zest refers to the colored part of lemon or other citrus peel, not the white pith underneath, which is usually bitter. A small kitchen tool called a zester easily removes the zest in long thin strips. (If you're using a zester and the recipe calls for grated or minced zest, finely chop the strips of zest with a heavy sharp knife.) You can also use the fine-holed side of a box grater; wrap plastic tightly around the grater before you begin, then, simply lift off the plastic when you're done—all the zest that normally ends up stuck in the grating holes will be on the plastic wrap. (Don't worry, you won't get any bits of plastic wrap in your zest.)

General Baking Tips

Home oven thermostats are notoriously inaccurate. To check yours, buy an oven thermometer (mercury thermometers are more expensive, but they are also more reliable than the spring type); if your thermostat is really off, you should have it recalibrated. In addition, most ovens have hot or cool spots, so you may find it necessary to turn baking pans or switch their positions half way through the baking time.

Check the recipe to see if there are any ingredients, such as butter, that should be at room temperature before beginning.

Preheat the oven for at least 15 minutes before baking. Glass conducts heat better than metal, so if you're using glass baking dishes (and the recipe doesn't specify glass), reduce the oven temperature by 25 degrees.

If the baking pan should be greased (see Cake Tips, page 66), do that before you start the recipe.

Assemble all the ingredients before you start making a dish. That way, you won't suddenly discover you're out of vanilla when you've already combined all the other ingredients for a batter.

Many recipes give a range of baking times, but because ovens differ, it's best to start checking baked goods for doneness a few minutes before the shortest time indicated.

Most cakes, pies and tarts, and cookies should be cooled on wire racks (in the pan or out, depending on the recipe) to prevent the bottom of the dessert from becoming soggy.

Special Techniques

TO BEAT EGG WHITES: When beating egg whites, make sure your bowl and beaters are clean and dry—even a speck of grease or the tiniest bit of egg yolk will prevent the whites from whipping to their greatest volume. Beat the whites on low speed just until foamy, then increase the speed to high and beat to soft or stiff peaks, as directed in the particular recipe. "Soft peaks" means the tips of the peaks of whites will fall over when the beaters are lifted out; "stiff peaks" will hold their shape. Be careful not to overbeat when making stiff peaks (they should never appear dry) or they will became coarse and grainy, and it will be difficult to fold or otherwise incorporate them into other ingredients. If you're adding sugar to the whites for a meringue, add it only gradually as you beat the whites—this gives the sugar a chance to dissolve and the whites a chance to reach their fullest volume. (There's less chance of overbeating when sugar is added to the whites.)

TO WHIP CREAM: For the best results, chill the beaters and the bowl you will be using and start with very cold cream. Beat on low speed until the cream starts to hold a shape, and to avoid splatters. Increase the speed to medium-high, then to high, and beat to soft or stiff peaks, as directed. Don't overbeat, or the cream will begin to turn to butter, developing small, unpleasant lumps. If you are beating cream to stiff peaks, reduce the mixer speed when the cream is almost at the right stage and beat on a lower speed until it forms stiff peaks.

TO FOLD IN INGREDIENTS: Ingredients such as beaten egg whites and whipped cream are often folded, rather than stirred, into a batter or mousse base to keep the texture light and airy. For most recipes, fold a small amount of the beaten whites (or cream) into the heavier or denser ingredients to lighten them, then fold in the remaining whites in several additions. To fold, use a large rubber spatula to spoon some of the whites onto the batter. With the edge of the spatula, cut down through the ingredients to the bottom of the bowl and then bring the mixture on the bottom up to the top of the bowl, rotating the bowl a quarter turn as you do so. Continue folding, giving the bowl a quarter turn each time, just until no streaks of white remain. Don't overdo it, or you'll deflate the batter.

Chapter One

fruit for all seasons

tropical fruit *medley*

creamy sugared *strawberries*

T HIS COLORFUL FRUIT SALAD COMBINES THE luscious flavors of perfectly ripe fruit with sweet coconut flakes. If you can, buy the fruit a few days ahead and keep it at room temperature until fragrant, being careful to not let it become overripe.

I small pineapple, peeled and cored

3 kiwis, peeled and thinly sliced

I cup diced mango

I cup diced papaya

3/4 cup sweetened shredded coconut

2 tablespoons dark rum

1. Cut the pineapple lengthwise into quarters, then cut each piece crosswise into 1/4-inch slices. Arrange the pineapple on a serving platter.

2. Arrange the kiwi slices decoratively over the pineapple, leaving a 1 1/2-inch border of pineapple visible.

3. In a small bowl, toss together the mango, papaya, and coconut. Scatter the mixture over the kiwi and pineapple slices. Sprinkle the rum evenly over the top.

4. Cover the salad with plastic wrap and refrigerate for at least 20 minutes before serving. To serve, spoon generous helpings into individual dessert bowls.

S E R V E S   6

N OTHING COULD BE SIMPLER TO MAKE THAN this creamy strawberry dessert, yet it is more sophisticated than you might imagine. Prepare it in a glass serving dish to show off the colorful layers, and serve in small portions—it's rich.

I quart small strawberries, hulled

I (15-ounce) container sour cream

1/4 cup plus 2 tablespoons packed dark
   brown sugar

1. Place the strawberries in a shallow 1-quart bowl, distributing them evenly. Using the back of a spoon or a rubber spatula, spread the sour cream in an even layer over the fruit. Sprinkle the brown sugar evenly on top of the cream. Cover with plastic wrap and refrigerate for at least 2 hours and up to 5 hours before serving.

2. To serve, spoon the strawberries, with their sour cream topping, into individual dessert bowls.

S E R V E S   6

summer *berry salad*

festive citrus *salad*

mIX AND MATCH THE BERRIES FOR THIS LIGHT summer dessert, choosing only those that are at their peak. If you can't find Chambord liqueur, use Grand Marnier or amaretto. These berries would also be good spooned over vanilla ice cream; in that case, the dish will serve six.

- 1 pint strawberries, hulled and halved or quartered if large
- 1 cup blueberries
- 1 cup raspberries
- 2 tablespoons Chambord (black raspberry liqueur)
- 1 tablespoon superfine sugar, or more to taste
- Crème fraîche (optional)

1. In a medium bowl, combine the berries, Chambord, and sugar. Cover with plastic wrap and refrigerate, stirring occasionally, for at least 1 hour and up to 6 hours before serving.

2. Spoon the berries and juices into dessert bowls and top each with a dollop of crème fraîche, if desired.

SERVES 4

iN THE WINTER MONTHS, WHEN GOOD FRESH fruit is often not available, this colorful citrus salad makes a light and refreshing ending to a meal.

- 1/2 cup sugar
- 1/2 cup water
- 1/3 cup dried cherries (about 2 ounces)
- 1 tablespoon Grand Marnier
- 4 seedless oranges
- 2 pink grapefruits
- 1/3 cup slivered blanched almonds
- Ground cinnamon, for sprinkling

1. In a medium saucepan, cook the sugar and water over medium heat for about 3 minutes, stirring until the sugar dissolves. Add the cherries and Grand Marnier and cook the syrup for about 5 minutes longer, without stirring, until thickened. Transfer the syrup to a bowl and let cool completely.

2. With a sharp knife, peel the oranges and slice crosswise. Repeat with the grapefruits. Arrange the fruit on a platter.

3. Sprinkle the almonds on top, then spoon the syrup and cherries evenly over the fruit. Cover with plastic wrap and refrigerate for at least 45 minutes before serving.

4. Sprinkle the fruit with cinnamon and serve immediately.

SERVES 6

autumn fruit *compote*

a COMPOTE IS A MIX OF FRUIT THAT HAS BEEN cooked gently in a sugar syrup to concentrate the flavors. Here we have enhanced a classic fall version with fragrant spices. For the best-tasting results, make it a few days in advance. Serve it topped with sour cream or spooned over sorbet or pound cake. (The whole spices are not meant to be eaten.)

2 cups red wine
1 cup water
1/3 cup sugar
2-inch piece cinnamon stick
2 whole cloves
1 bay leaf
4 large plums, pitted and cut in
**   1/2-inch-thick wedges**
3 large pears, cored and cut in
**   1/2-inch-thick wedges**
2 cups seedless red grapes
1 cup dried figs, cut in 1/2-inch-thick pieces
1 cup dried apricots, halved

1. In a large saucepan over high heat, combine the wine, water, sugar, cinnamon, cloves, and bay leaf. Bring the mixture to a boil over high heat and cook for 2 minutes, stirring to dissolve the sugar. Let the mixture cook for 5 minutes longer, without stirring, until the syrup thickens slightly.

2. Add the plums, pears, grapes, figs, and apricots and reduce the heat to medium-low. Cook for about 12 minutes, stirring occasionally, until tender. Remove the pan from the heat and let cool.

3. The compote can be served warm or cold in individual dessert bowls.

SERVES 8

QUEEN OF THE KITCHEN TIP

Selecting Fruit

Although it's fun to get raspberries in the dead of winter, the best fruit is what's *really* in season and at its peak, from the first berries of spring to autumn's juicy pears.

If you can get locally grown fruit, at a farmers' market or roadside stand, so much the better. In general, look for fruit with good color and that feels heavy for its size. Avoid any that is bruised or blemished (although the rough brown spots on some varieties of apples, called russeting, are not an indication of spoilage). Ripe fruit usually has a delicious fragrance—although it can be difficult to tell with melons so ask at the produce counter for help. But just as you don't want hard, under-ripe fruit, you usually should avoid soft, overripe fruit. Most slightly underripe fruit will ripen at room temperature; refrigerated, it will not ripen any further.

FRUIT FOR ALL
SEASONS

brown-sugar baked apples

THIS OLD-FASHIONED DESSERT GIVES OFF AN irresistible cinnamon-sweet scent as it bakes. Put it in the oven just before dinner and you can be sure that everyone will save room for dessert!

6 medium baking apples, such as Granny Smith

2/3 cup water

1/2 cup packed dark brown sugar

1 strip orange or lemon zest (removed with a vegetable peeler)

Pinch of salt

1/2 teaspoon ground cinnamon

2 tablespoons unsalted butter, cut in pieces

1. Preheat the oven to 350°F.

2. Core the apples and peel them to about halfway down from the top. Place them, peeled-side up, in a 13- x 9-inch baking dish. Set aside.

3. In a small saucepan, combine the water, brown sugar, zest, and salt. Bring the mixture to a simmer over medium-high heat and cook, stirring, for 2 minutes. Stir in the cinnamon.

4. Pour the syrup over the apples, then scatter the butter pieces over the top. Cover the dish with foil and bake the apples, basting them every 15 minutes, for about 1 hour, until they are tender when pierced with a knife. Serve warm, or refrigerate and serve cold.

SERVES 6

spiced poached *pears*

tENDER, RIPE PEARS BECOME DELECTABLE when poached in this white wine syrup. Ginger and black peppercorns impart a subtle, warm spiciness to the fruit. Serve this simple dish alone or alongside pound cake or Classic Angel Food Cake (page 78) for a stunning dessert.

1 (750-ml) bottle white wine

1 cup sugar

1 vanilla bean, sliced lengthwise

1-inch piece cinnamon stick

1 slice (1/2-inch-thick) fresh ginger

5 black peppercorns

8 firm pears

1. In a large heavy saucepan, combine the wine, sugar, vanilla, cinnamon, ginger, and peppercorns over high heat. Bring the liquid to a simmer and cook for 5 to 6 minutes, stirring occasionally, until the sugar dissolves and the liquid thickens slightly.

2. Meanwhile, peel, halve, and core the pears. Reduce the heat to medium and add the pears to the cooking liquid. Cook for 12 to 15 minutes, until the pears are tender when pierced with a knife and the liquid is reduced to a syrup.

3. Remove from the heat and, with a slotted spoon, transfer the pears to a large serving bowl; strain the syrup over the top of the pears. Cover with plastic wrap and refrigerate until serving time.

4. To serve, spoon the pear halves into individual dessert bowls and drizzle some of the sauce on top.

SERVES 8

golden cherry *fritters*

 OU MAY NOT THINK OF FRYING CHERRIES, but the contrast between the crunchy golden fritter and the juicy sweet cherries in this recipe is sublime. For best results, don't overcrowd the pan while frying, since the oil must maintain a constant temperature. Lower the cherries gently into the oil, away from you, to avoid splattering.

2 large eggs, separated

1 1/4 cups all-purpose flour

1 cup white wine

3 tablespoons granulated sugar

Pinch of salt

12 ounces sweet cherries with stems

Vegetable oil, for deep frying

2 tablespoons confectioners' sugar, for sprinkling

1 teaspoon ground cinnamon, for sprinkling

1. In a medium bowl, whisk together the egg yolks, flour, wine, 1 tablespoon granulated sugar, and the salt to make a smooth batter. Cover the batter with plastic wrap and refrigerate for 30 minutes.

2. Rinse the cherries and drain them thoroughly on paper towels. Tie the cherries together by the stems with kitchen string in bunches of 3 or 4 and set aside.

3. In a large, deep saucepan, heat the oil to 350°F (small bubbles form around a wooden spoon when inserted into the oil).

4. In another medium bowl, beat the egg whites with an electric mixer until foamy. Add the remaining 2 tablespoons granulated sugar and continue to beat until the mixture is stiff and glossy. Using a rubber spatula, gently fold the egg-white mixture into the yolk mixture.

5. Thread one cherry bunch at a time onto the prongs of a long-handled fork. Dip the cherries into the batter and allow the excess to drip off. Lower the cherries into the hot oil, slip off the fork, and fry for 2 minutes, or until golden brown. Work in batches so as not to crowd the saucepan.

6. Remove the cherries with a slotted spoon and drain on paper towels.

7. In a small bowl, mix together the confectioners' sugar and cinnamon. Place the mixture in a sifter and sprinkle a generous amount over the cherries. Serve immediately.

SERVES 4

fresh berry parfaits
with lemon cream

TRY ALTERNATING LAYERS OF DIFFERENT jewel-toned berries with the luscious lemon cream in this beautiful dessert. Tall, narrow parfait glasses are indeed best for this, but wineglasses also work nicely.

LEMON CREAM

5 large egg yolks

1/2 cup sugar

Grated zest of 2 lemons

1/2 cup fresh lemon juice (from about 2 lemons)

1/4 cup (1/2 stick) unsalted butter, at
　　room temperature

1 cup heavy cream

1 cup fresh blackberries or blueberries

1 cup fresh raspberries or quartered strawberries,
　　plus additional for garnish

1. Make the lemon cream. In a medium bowl or in the top of a double boiler (not suspended over water yet), whisk together the egg yolks and sugar until thick and light in color. Whisk in the lemon zest and juice.

2. Suspend the bowl over simmering water and whisk for about 10 minutes, or until the mixture starts to thicken. Add the butter, 1 tablespoon at a time, and continue to whisk for about 5 minutes, until the mixture is thick. (It will continue to thicken as it cools.) Let the mixture cool transfer to a container with a tight-fitting lid and refrigerate for at least 4 hours.

3. In a large bowl, whip the cream with an electric mixer until soft peaks form. Using a rubber spatula, carefully fold the lemon mixture into the whipped cream.

4. Divide the blackberries among 8 parfait glasses. Top with half of the lemon cream, then with the raspberries, and finally with the remaining lemon cream. Garnish with additional raspberries and serve immediately or cover with plastic wrap and refrigerate for up to 8 hours.

SERVES 8

sweet tart
cherry sauce

nutmeg
pear sauce

hERE, DRIED CHERRIES ARE SIMMERED WITH sugar and water to make a versatile fruit sauce that complements anything from cheesecake to pound cake to ice cream. This sauce keeps well in the refrigerator for several days; to serve, reheat gently, stirring occasionally with a wooden spoon.

I cup water

3/4 cup sugar

3/4 cup dried sour cherries (about 4 ounces)

I tablespoon kirsch (optional)

1. In a small heavy saucepan, combine the water and sugar and bring to a boil over medium-high heat, stirring to dissolve the sugar. Reduce the heat to medium-low, add the cherries, and cook for about 15 minutes, until they are plump and soft. Remove from the heat and stir in the kirsch, if desired. Let the sauce cool.

2. Serve warm, at room temperature, or slightly chilled.

MAKES ABOUT I 1/4 CUPS

tHIS FRAGRANT SAUCE IS ESPECIALLY DELICIOUS alongside quick breads, plain cakes, or fritters, topped with a cloud of freshly made whipped cream.

8 pears, peeled, cored, and chopped

2 tablespoons fresh lemon juice

2 tablespoons water

2 tablespoons sugar

I-inch piece cinnamon stick or

1/2 teaspoon ground

1/2 teaspoon freshly grated nutmeg

1. In a large saucepan, combine the pears, lemon juice, water, sugar, cinnamon, and nutmeg. Set over medium heat and bring the mixture to a simmer. Partially cover the pan and simmer, stirring occasionally, for about 20 minutes, until the pears are soft and saucelike.

2. Transfer the sauce to a large bowl and let it cool to room temperature. Cover with plastic wrap and refrigerate for at least 2 hours. Remove the cinnamon stick before serving.

SERVES 4 TO 6

Chapter Two

comforting crisps & cobblers

apple pandowdy

SOFT-BAKED APPLES ARE CROWNED WITH SWEET, crunchy squares of buttery cinnamon toast in this old-fashioned dessert.

2 tablespoons granulated sugar,
   plus more for sprinkling

1 teaspoon ground cinnamon

12 thin slices white bread, crusts removed

6 tablespoons (3/4 stick) unsalted butter, melted

6 to 7 baking apples, such as Jonathan or Rome,
   peeled, cored, and cut in 1/2-inch-thick slices

1/4 cup molasses

2 tablespoons brown sugar

1/2 teaspoon ground cardamom

1/8 teaspoon freshly grated nutmeg

Pinch of salt

Sour cream or whipped cream, for serving (optional)

1. Preheat the oven to 375°F.

2. In a small bowl, combine 2 tablespoons granulated sugar and the cinnamon. Sprinkle 1 tablespoon of the cinnamon-sugar evenly over the bottom of an ungreased 11 3/4- x 7 1/2-inch baking pan.

3. Using a pastry brush, coat both sides of each slice of bread with melted butter. Line the bottom of the prepared pan with 6 slices of bread, turning them to coat both sides with the cinnamon-sugar.

4. Put the apple slices in a large bowl and add the molasses, brown sugar, cardamom, nutmeg, and salt, tossing well to coat evenly. Spoon the apple mixture into the prepared pan, including all the juices.

5. Cut the remaining 6 bread slices into quarters. Lay on top of the apple mixture and sprinkle with the remaining cinnamon-sugar. Sprinkle the bread with additional granulated sugar, if desired.

6. Bake the pandowdy for 50 to 60 minutes, until the filling is bubbling, the apples are tender, and the bread is well toasted. Let cool slightly on a wire rack before serving. Serve warm, topped with sour cream or whipped cream, if desired.

SERVES 8

cinnamon apple *crumble*

ERE'S THE PERFECT COMFORT FOOD, EQUALLY good served warm from the oven or cold from the refrigerator. The ginger in the topping accents the apples and cinnamon, bringing out their earthy-sweetness. For an extra special treat, this autumnal dessert can be served with vanilla ice cream or frozen yogurt.

CINNAMON-GINGER TOPPING

3/4 cup all-purpose flour

3/4 cup packed dark brown sugar

1 teaspoon ground cinnamon

1 teaspoon ground ginger

Pinch of salt

6 tablespoons (3/4 stick) cold unsalted butter, cut in pieces

APPLE FILLING

5 baking apples, such as Granny Smith, peeled, cored, and sliced

1/4 cup granulated sugar

1 tablespoon fresh lemon juice

1/2 teaspoon ground cinnamon

1. Preheat the oven to 375°F.

2. Make the cinnamon-ginger topping. In a medium bowl, toss together the flour, brown sugar, cinnamon, ginger, and salt. Using your fingers, rub the butter into the flour mixture until the mixture resembles coarse crumbs. Set the mixture aside.

3. Make the apple filling. In a large bowl, toss the apples with the granulated sugar, lemon juice, and cinnamon, mixing well. Pour the apple mixture into an ungreased 13- x 9-inch baking pan. Sprinkle the cinnamon-ginger topping evenly on top.

4. Bake the crumble for 40 minutes, or until the apples are tender. Let the crumble cool on a wire rack for at least 20 minutes before serving.

SERVES 6

blackberry *cobbler*

CRISPS AND COBBLERS HAIL FROM A CLOSE-KNIT family of desserts, which also includes slumps, grunts, crumbles, and betties. All of these treats rely on plenty of juicy, ripe fruit to be baked under a pastry-like topping. While crisps, as the name suggests, have a nubby, crunchy topping, cobblers have a flakier, biscuit cap. Here we have added heavy cream to the batter to make the biscuit topping even richer and more scrumptious.

BISCUIT TOPPING

1 1/2 cups all-purpose flour

3/4 cup sugar

2 teaspoons baking powder

1/2 teaspoon salt

6 tablespoons (3/4 stick) cold unsalted butter, cut in pieces

3/4 cup heavy cream

BLACKBERRY FILLING

4 cups fresh or frozen blackberries

1/2 cup sugar

1 1/2 tablespoons all-purpose flour

1/8 teaspoon ground allspice

1. Preheat the oven to 375°F.

2. Make the biscuit topping. In a large bowl, toss together the flour, sugar, baking powder, and salt. Using your fingers, rub the butter into the flour mixture until the mixture resembles coarse crumbs.

3. Add the cream to the crumbs, tossing with a fork until a soft batter forms. Set the topping aside.

4. Make the blackberry filling. In a large bowl, toss together the blackberries, sugar, flour, and allspice. Spoon the filling into an ungreased 13- x 9-inch baking pan. Using a large spoon, drop mounds of the biscuit topping on the blackberry filling (the batter will spread as it cooks).

5. Bake the cobbler for 45 minutes, or until the topping is golden brown and the filling is bubbling. Let the cobbler cool slightly on a wire rack before serving. Serve warm or at room temperature.

SERVES 6

ginger peach *cobbler*

RANDY AND GINGER ADD A GROWN-UP TOUCH to this childhood favorite. You do not need to add a lot of either of them; just a hint of flavor perfectly accents the peaches. If peaches aren't in season, you can use frozen ones, but don't defrost them before baking or they will fall apart.

GINGER TOPPING

1 1/2 cups all-purpose flour

3/4 cup granulated sugar

1 tablespoon baking powder

1/2 teaspoon ground ginger

1/2 teaspoon salt

6 tablespoons (3/4 stick) cold unsalted butter,
   cut in pieces

3/4 cup milk

PEACH-BRANDY FILLING

6 medium peaches, pitted and sliced
   or 6 cups frozen sliced peaches

1/4 cup packed light brown sugar

1 1/2 tablespoons all-purpose flour

1 tablespoon brandy (optional)

1 teaspoon ground ginger

2 tablespoons cold unsalted butter, cut in pieces

1. Preheat the oven to 375°F.

2. Make the ginger topping. In a large bowl, toss together the flour, granulated sugar, baking powder, ginger, and salt. Using your fingers, rub the butter into the flour mixture until the mixture resembles coarse crumbs.

3. Add the milk to the crumbs, tossing with a fork until a soft batter forms. Set the topping aside.

4. Make the peach-brandy filling. In a large bowl, toss together the peaches, brown sugar, flour, brandy, if using, and ginger. Spoon the filling into an ungreased 13- x 9-inch baking pan. Dot the top with the butter pieces.

5. Using a large spoon, drop mounds of the ginger topping on the fruit filling. Bake the cobbler for 45 minutes, or until the top is golden brown and the filling is bubbling. Let the cobbler cool slightly on a wire rack before serving. Serve warm or at room temperature.

SERVES 6

raspberry nectarine almond crisp

OASTED ALMONDS ADD A WONDERFUL CRUNCH to the crumble topping of this sweet and juicy fruit dessert. Be careful when toasting the almonds, since they burn easily; you want them to just release their oils and get slightly brown.

CRUNCHY-ALMOND TOPPING

1/2 cup sliced natural almonds

3/4 cup all-purpose flour

1/4 cup granulated sugar

1/4 cup packed light brown sugar

1/8 teaspoon ground cinnamon

Pinch of salt

6 tablespoons (3/4 stick) cold unsalted butter, cut in pieces

RASPBERRY-NECTARINE FILLING

9 medium nectarines, pitted and sliced

1 cup raspberries

1 1/2 tablespoons all-purpose flour

1/4 cup granulated sugar

1. Preheat the oven to 375°F.

2. Make the crunchy-almond topping. Arrange the almonds in a single layer on a baking sheet and toast them in the oven for 3 minutes, or until pale golden. Let them cool completely on a wire rack. Chop coarsely.

3. In a medium bowl, toss together the flour, granulated sugar, brown sugar, cinnamon, and salt. Using your fingers, rub the butter into the flour mixture until it resembles coarse crumbs. Add the almonds, tossing well to incorporate. Set the topping aside.

4. Make the raspberry-nectarine filling. In a large bowl, toss the nectarine slices with the raspberries, flour, and granulated sugar. Pour the mixture into an ungreased 13- x 9-inch pan. Sprinkle the crunchy-almond topping evenly on top.

5. Bake the crisp for 40 minutes, or until the nectarines are tender. Let the crisp cool on a wire rack for at least 20 minutes before serving. Serve warm or at room temperature.

SERVES 6

pear ginger *duff*

A N AIRY, GINGER-FLAVORED SPONGE CAKE TOPS poached pears in this modern adaptation of the Early American cobbler. The cake completely covers the pears, which allows them to cook further, so don't over-cook them initially; 8 minutes is the maximum time, depending in the ripeness of the fruit.

POACHED PEARS

1 cup white wine

1/2 cup granulated sugar

2 tablespoons quick-cooking tapioca

6 pears, peeled, cored, and sliced

1 teaspoon grated lemon zest

GINGER CAKE

2/3 cup granulated sugar

4 large eggs, separated

2 teaspoons vanilla extract

1 teaspoon ground ginger

1/2 cup all-purpose flour, sifted

Confectioners' sugar, for dusting

1. Preheat the oven to 350°F. Grease a shallow 2 1/2-quart casserole or a 10-inch cake pan.

2. Make the poached pears. In a large saucepan, bring the wine, granulated sugar, and tapioca to a boil over high heat. Stir in the pears and lemon zest and return the mixture to a boil. Cover the pan, reduce the heat to medium-low, and sim-

mer gently for 8 minutes, or until the fruit has softened slightly. Spoon the mixture into the casserole and set aside.

3. Make the ginger cake. In a large bowl, beat the granulated sugar and egg yolks with an electric mixer until pale and thick, 3 to 4 minutes. Beat in the vanilla and ginger.

4. In a large bowl, using clean beaters, beat the egg whites at high speed until soft peaks form. Using a rubber spatula, gently fold the flour into the whites, then fold this mixture into the beaten egg yolk mixture. Pour the batter over the pears in the casserole and smooth the top.

5. Bake the duff for 35 minutes, or until the ginger cake is golden brown and begins to pull away from the side of the casserole. Let cool slightly on a wire rack for 10 minutes. Dust with confectioners' sugar and serve warm.

SERVES 6 TO 8

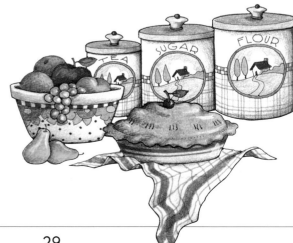

raspberry blueberry *grunt*

COMFORTING
CRISPS & COBBLERS

DON'T BE PUT OFF BY ITS NAME—A GRUNT tastes a lot better than it sounds. It's an old-time American fruit dessert falling somewhere in between a cobbler and a dumpling. Serve it warm from the oven with whipped cream or small scoops of vanilla ice cream on top.

BERRY FILLING

2 cups blueberries

2 cups raspberries

1/2 cup sugar

1/4 cup water

1-inch piece cinnamon stick

SOUR CREAM BISCUITS

1 cup all-purpose flour

2 tablespoons sugar

1 teaspoon baking powder

1/2 teaspoon baking soda

1/4 teaspoon salt

2 tablespoons cold unsalted butter,
   cut in pieces

1/2 cup sour cream

2 teaspoons granulated sugar, for sprinkling

1/4 teaspoon freshly grated nutmeg,
   for sprinkling

1. Preheat the oven to 350°F.

2. Make the berry filling. In a medium saucepan over high heat, stir together the blueberries, raspberries, sugar, water, and cinnamon and bring to a boil. Reduce the heat to medium and let simmer, uncovered, for 5 minutes. Remove the cinnamon and pour the mixture into an ungreased 9-inch cake pan and set aside.

3. Make the sour cream biscuits. In a food processor, combine the flour, sugar, baking powder, baking soda, and salt and pulse to combine. Add the butter and pulse until the mixture resembles coarse crumbs. Add the sour cream and pulse just until a ball of dough forms.

4. Using your hands, form 1-inch balls of dough and drop them onto the berry mixture. Sprinkle the top of the grunt with the remaining 2 teaspoons sugar and nutmeg.

5. Cover the grunt with foil and bake for 15 minutes. Remove the foil and bake for an additional 10 minutes. Let cool slightly on a wire rack and serve warm.

SERVES 4 TO 6

strawberry chocolate *shortcakes*

CRISP, BUTTERY, CHOCOLATE-FLAVORED biscuits are a marvelous partner for juicy, ripe strawberries in this pretty dessert that would be the perfect ending for a summer brunch or lunch.

CHOCOLATE SHORTCAKES

1 cup all-purpose flour

1/2 cup granulated sugar

1/4 cup unsweetened cocoa powder

1 1/2 teaspoons baking powder

1 teaspoon baking soda

1/4 teaspoon salt

5 tablespoons unsalted butter, melted

1/3 cup milk

STRAWBERRY FILLING

1 quart fresh strawberries, hulled and halved

1/3 cup granulated sugar

1 teaspoon vanilla extract

3/4 cup heavy cream

Confectioners' sugar, for dusting

1. Make the chocolate shortcakes. Preheat the oven to 425°F.

2. In a medium bowl, combine the flour, granulated sugar, cocoa, baking powder, baking soda, and salt. Add the butter and milk, and stir just until a soft dough forms.

3. Drop the batter onto an ungreased baking sheet in 4 equal mounds. Bake for 12 to 15 minutes, until a toothpick inserted in the centers comes out clean. Transfer the sheet to a wire rack and let the shortcakes cool.

4. Make the strawberry filling. In a medium bowl, mash 1/4 cup of the strawberries with a fork. Stir in the remaining strawberries, granulated sugar, and vanilla, and let stand for 20 minutes.

5. In a medium bowl, beat the cream with an electric mixer until stiff peaks form.

6. Using a serrated knife, carefully slice the cooled shortcakes in half horizontally. Place each shortcake bottom on a serving plate and spoon whipped cream and strawberry filling on top. Cover with the shortcake tops. Dust with confectioners' sugar and serve immediately.

SERVES 4

apricot cherry *turnovers*

THESE FLAKY, FRUIT-FILLED TURNOVERS ARE AS good for brunch as they are for dessert. Packaged puff pastry makes them very simple to prepare.

1 (15-ounce) can apricots in light syrup,
   halved and pitted
3/4 cup halved and pitted bing cherries
1/4 cup granulated sugar
1 tablespoon instant tapioca
1/4 teaspoon almond extract
1 (17 1/4-ounce) package frozen puff pastry,
   thawed according to package directions
1 large egg, beaten
Confectioners' sugar, for dusting

1. Preheat the oven to 400°F. Grease two baking sheets.

2. In a medium bowl, combine the apricots, cherries, granulated sugar, tapioca, and almond extract. Set the mixture aside for 20 minutes.

3. Unfold one sheet of puff pastry onto a lightly floured surface and roll it out into a 12-inch square. Cut the square into 4 equal squares. Divide half of the fruit filling among the pastry squares, placing mounds in the center of each square. Moisten the edges of the pastry, fold over to form triangles, and pinch to seal. Repeat with the remaining puff pastry and fruit mixture.

4. Using a pastry brush, lightly coat the turnovers with the beaten egg.

5. Place the turnovers on the prepared baking sheets and bake for 25 minutes, or until the pastry is golden brown. Let the sheets cool slightly on wire racks. Dust the turnovers heavily with confectioners' sugar and serve immediately.

SERVES 8

QUEEN OF THE KITCHEN TIP

Decorating Turnovers

Turnovers are wonderfully versatile. Not only can you vary the filling, but you can also dress them up very simply with a little Royal Icing:

Beat 1 large egg white, 1 cup confectioners' sugar, and 1 teaspoon fresh lemon juice with an electric mixer for 8 minutes, or until the icing is thick enough to hold its shape. Gradually add additional confectioners' sugar if needed. Using a fork, drizzle the icing over the slightly warm turnovers and serve.

Chapter Three
homey pies & elegant tarts

 # Crust Tips

Making piecrusts sometimes intimidates people. In fact, it is not difficult to make good flaky pastry if you follow these tips:

- All your cold ingredients must come right from the refrigerator. This is essential for a flaky crust: The fat should melt in the oven to form the layers of flaky pastry, not while the dough is being rolled out. Prepare your cold ingredients ahead of time and keep them in the refrigerator until you are ready. This includes cutting up the butter and shortening. Some people even go so far as to chill all their ingredients, including the flour and sugar, and their equipment. This is not necessary if you work quickly in a cool area (not next to a hot oven).

- We call for ice water in our pie pastry to keep the temperature of the pastry down, which renders the most flaky crust. The best method is to put three ice cubes into the measuring cup and fill the measuring cup to the desired amount as soon as you start assembling your ingredients. By the time you're ready, all the ice will have melted away, leaving just ice water. (If some pieces of the ice remain, use a measuring spoon to add the water, avoiding the pieces of ice. Don't let pieces of ice mix into the pastry, or you'll end up with soggy spots.)

- Next to your fingertips, a pastry blender is the best tool for cutting butter and/or shortening into the flour mixture. If you don't have one, use two knives. Place the butter on top of the flour mixture and, holding one knife in each hand, cut the butter in opposite directions.

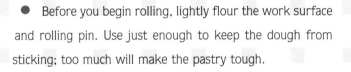

The result should be a coarse meal, approximately the size of peas. Don't overwork the dough—you want small pieces of butter in your dough; this is what makes it flaky.

- Once the pastry comes together, wrap it in plastic, not foil, and allow it to rest for 30 minutes in the refrigerator. If you refrigerate it longer, give the pastry a minute or so to warm up before rolling out. Some of our recipes call for only half a recipe of pastry. In this case, you can freeze the remaining half of the pastry for use later. To defrost, leave it in the refrigerator overnight, and let it rest on the counter for 8 to 15 minutes before rolling out.

- Before you begin rolling, lightly flour the work surface and rolling pin. Use just enough to keep the dough from sticking; too much will make the pastry tough.

- Roll out the pastry dough quickly. Work from the middle outwards and move the pastry around to keep it from sticking to the work surface. When making pies, roll the pastry approximately 3 inches larger than the pie plate. For tarts, roll the pastry approximately 2 inches larger than the pan.

- To transfer the pastry from the board to the pie or tart pan, roll the pastry around a very well floured rolling pin. Transfer to the pie plate, unrolling the pastry over the plate. If there are any holes or cracks, press scraps of dough into the pastry to seal them.

flaky. *pie pastry*

sweet *tart crust*

tHIS VERSATILE PASTRY CAN BE USED FOR all your pies. To ensure a flaky, tender crust, chill all your ingredients and do not overwork the dough. It can be frozen for up to one month (wrap it well in plastic wrap, then heavy duty foil).

- 2 2/3 cups all-purpose flour
- 2 tablespoons sugar
- 1/2 teaspoon salt
- 3/4 cup (1 1/2 sticks) cold unsalted butter, cut in 1/2-inch pieces
- 1/4 cup vegetable shortening, cut in 4 pieces
- 5 to 6 tablespoons ice water

1. In a medium bowl, combine the flour, sugar, and salt. Using a pastry blender, two knives, or your fingertips, cut in the butter and shortening until the mixture resembles coarse meal. Drizzle 5 tablespoons ice water over the top, tossing the mixture with a fork until the dough just comes together. If necessary, add up to 1 tablespoon more water.

2. Divide the dough in half and shape each half into a disk. Wrap in plastic and refrigerate for at least 30 minutes or overnight.

MAKES PASTRY FOR ONE DOUBLE-CRUST 9-INCH PIE

a GOOD TART CRUST IS RICH, DELICATE, AND crumbly—not flaky like pie pastry. It's more like a sugar cookie. It's not easily harmed, so you don't have to handle the dough too gingerly.

- 1 cup plus 2 tablespoons all-purpose flour
- 1 tablespoon sugar
- 1/4 teaspoon salt
- 1/2 cup (1 stick) cold unsalted butter, cut in pieces
- 1 large egg yolk
- 1 teaspoon vanilla extract
- 1 tablespoon water, if needed

1. In a large bowl, toss together the flour, sugar, and salt. Using a pastry blender, two knives, or your fingertips, cut in the butter until the mixture resembles coarse meal.

2. In a small bowl, mix together the egg yolk and vanilla. Add the egg mixture to the flour mixture and mix the dough with a rubber spatula or your hands until it holds together. If the dough seems too crumbly, add the extra water. Shape the dough into a disk and wrap in plastic. Refrigerate for 30 minutes or overnight.

MAKES PASTRY FOR ONE 9-INCH TART

country fair
apple pie

WHO DOESN'T LOVE APPLE PIE? AND HERE the traditional combination of cinnamon and nutmeg is sure to please apple pie fans of all ages. The best apples to use for this pie are Granny Smith, but you could also try other varieties, such as Empire or McIntosh.

5 large baking apples, peeled, cored, and sliced

1/2 cup sugar

2 tablespoons cornstarch

1 tablespoon fresh lemon juice

1/4 teaspoon ground cinnamon

1/8 teaspoon freshly grated nutmeg

1 recipe Flaky Pie Pastry (p. 37)

1 large egg

1 tablespoon water

1. Preheat the oven to 425°F.

2. In a medium bowl, mix together the apple slices, sugar, cornstarch, lemon juice, cinnamon, and nutmeg. Set the mixture aside.

3. On a lightly floured surface, roll out one of the dough halves to a 12 1/2-inch round. Fit the dough into a 9-inch pie plate.

4. On a lightly floured surface, roll out the remaining dough to a 10-inch round.

5. Spoon the apple mixture into the pie shell. Cover with the top crust, crimping the edges to seal tightly.

6. In a small bowl, whisk together the egg and water. Brush the top of the pie with the egg-water glaze. Using a small sharp knife, cut four steam vents in the top of the crust.

7. Bake the pie for 10 minutes, then lower the heat to 350°F and bake for about 45 minutes, until the crust is golden brown and the filling is bubbling. Let the pie cool on a wire rack. Serve warm or at room temperature.

SERVES 8

QUEEN OF THE KITCHEN TIP

Decorating the Crust

Instead of just cutting slits in the crust with a knife, you can use small decorative cutters to make the steam vents. After rolling out the top crust, use a very small cutter—perhaps an apple shape for this pie, or a star— to make three or four evenly spaced cutouts in the crust, then transfer the crust to the top of the pie. You can reserve the cutouts to decorate the crust too, if you like—brush them lightly on one side with water to "glue" them to the crust.

strawberry-rhubarb *crumb pie*

S WEET JUICY STRAWBERRIES AND TENDER stalks of young spring rhubarb make a delicious filling for this oatmeal crumb–topped pie. If fresh rhubarb isn't in season, you can use frozen, which is available in some large supermarkets. Here we call for only half a recipe of Flaky Pie Pastry: the remaining pastry will keep in the freezer, tightly wrapped in plastic, for one month.

STRAWBERRY-RHUBARB FILLING

I pound rhubarb, red stalks only, trimmed and cubed

I pint strawberries, hulled and halved if large

I cup granulated sugar

2 tablespoons instant tapioca

OATMEAL CRUMB TOPPING

1/3 cup packed brown sugar

1/4 cup all-purpose flour

1/4 cup rolled oats

1/2 teaspoon ground ginger

1/4 cup (1/2 stick) unsalted butter, cut in small pieces and slightly softened

1/2 recipe Flaky Pie Pastry (p. 37)

1. Preheat the oven to 350°F.

2. Make the strawberry-rhubarb filling. In a large bowl, mix together the rhubarb, strawberries, granulated sugar, and tapioca and toss well. Let sit for about 20 minutes, until the tapioca softens somewhat.

3. Meanwhile, make the oatmeal crumb topping. In a large bowl, combine the brown sugar, flour, oats, and ginger and mix well. Using your fingers, rub the butter into the oatmeal mixture until the mixture resembles coarse crumbs.

4. On a lightly floured surface, roll out the dough to a 12 1/2-inch round. Fit the dough into a 9-inch pie plate. Trim the overhanging dough even with the edge of the pie pan.

5. Spoon the strawberry-rhubarb filling into the pie shell. Sprinkle the oatmeal crumb topping evenly on top.

6. Bake the pie for about 50 minutes, until the topping is golden and the filling is bubbling. Let the pie cool on a wire rack. Serve the pie warm or at room temperature, or refrigerate and serve chilled.

SERVES 8

cherry pie

A TRADITIONAL WOVEN LATTICE TOP IS NOT difficult to make, but here we give instructions for an easy streamlined version. Vanilla ice cream is the classic accompaniment, but by all means choose your favorite "à la mode."

CHERRY FILLING

1 cup sugar

3 tablespoons cornstarch

Pinch of salt

2 (16-ounce) cans pitted tart cherries in water, drained and 1/3 cup juice reserved

1 teaspoon fresh lemon juice

1 recipe Flaky Pie Pastry (p. 37)

2 tablespoons unsalted butter, cut in pieces

1. Place a large sheet of foil on the bottom of the oven to catch any drips. Position a rack in the lower third of the oven and preheat the oven to 400°F.

2. Make the cherry filling. In a large bowl, combine the sugar, cornstarch, and salt and stir until well blended. Add the cherries, their reserved juice, and the lemon juice and stir until thoroughly combined. Set aside at room temperature.

3. On a lightly floured surface, roll out one of the dough disks to a 12 1/2-inch round. Fit the dough into a 9-inch glass pie plate. Trim the overhanging dough even with the edge of the pie pan. Refrigerate.

4. On the lightly floured surface, roll out the remaining dough to a 12-inch round. Using a ruler as a guide, cut the round into twelve 3/4-inch-wide strips using a pastry wheel.

5. Spoon the cherry filling into the pie shell and dot with the butter. Moisten the edge of the pie shell with water. Lay 6 of the lattice strips evenly across the pie. Lay the remaining strips across them, either at right angles or on the diagonal. Trim the edges of the strips even with the edge of the pie shell. With the back of a fork, crimp the edge to seal the ends of the strips and form a decorative border.

6. Bake the pie for 55 to 60 minutes, until the juices are bubbling and the crust is golden brown. If the edge of the crust starts to brown too much, cover it with strips of foil. Let the pie cool completely on a wire rack. Serve at room temperature, or refrigerate and serve chilled.

SERVES 8

42

cranberry-*pear pie*

A MIX OF FRESH AND DRIED CRANBERRIES gives this special pie extra texture. This makes a colorful holiday dessert, but it is easy enough to prepare for a casual dinner with friends.

1 recipe Flaky Pie Pastry (p. 37)

3 large pears, peeled, cored, and sliced

1 1/2 cups fresh or frozen cranberries (about 5 ounces)

3/4 cup sugar

1/2 cup dried cranberries (about 3 ounces)

2 tablespoons cornstarch

1 teaspoon grated lemon zest

1/2 teaspoon ground ginger

1 tablespoon milk

1. Preheat the oven to 425°F.

2. On a lightly floured surface, roll out one of the dough halves to a 12 1/2-inch round. Fit the dough into a 9-inch pie plate. Trim the overhanging dough even with the edge of the pie pan. Refrigerate.

3. On a lightly floured surface, roll out the remaining dough to a 10-inch round.

4. In a medium bowl, mix together the pears, fresh cranberries, sugar, dried cranberries, cornstarch, lemon zest, and ginger.

5. Place the cranberry-pear mixture into the pie shell. Cover the fruit mixture with the top crust, crimping the edge to seal.

Brush the top of the pie with the milk. Using a small sharp knife, cut four steam vents in the top of the crust.

6. Bake the pie for 10 minutes, then lower the heat to 350°F and continue to bake for about 45 minutes, until the crust is golden brown and the fruit filling is bubbling. Let the pie cool on a wire rack. Serve warm or at room temperature.

SERVES 8

chocolate orange
meringue pie

HERE ARE TWO SURPRISES IN THIS MERINGUE pie: an orange filling instead of the traditional lemon, and a "black bottom," a delicious thin layer of chocolate between the filling and the crust.

1/2 recipe **Flaky Pie Pastry (p. 37)**

2 ounces semisweet chocolate, finely grated

ZESTY ORANGE FILLING

1 1/2 cups sugar

1/3 cup cornstarch

1/4 teaspoon salt

1 1/2 cups cold water

2 tablespoons grated orange zest

1/3 cup fresh orange juice

3 large egg yolks, beaten

2 tablespoons unsalted butter, cut in pieces

MERINGUE TOPPING

4 large egg whites, at room temperature

1/2 cup sugar

Pinch of salt

1. On a lightly floured surface, roll out the dough to a 12 1/2-inch round. Fit the dough into a 9-inch pie plate. Trim the edge of the dough, leaving a 1/2-inch overhang. Fold the excess dough under itself and crimp the edge. Refrigerate for 30 minutes.

2. Preheat the oven to 375°F.

3. Line the pie shell with foil and fill with dried beans or rice. Bake for 15 minutes. Remove the foil and beans and bake for 8 to 10 minutes longer, until the shell is golden brown. Transfer the pie shell to a wire rack. Sprinkle the grated chocolate evenly over the bottom of the pie shell.

4. Make the zesty orange filling. In a large heavy saucepan, whisk together the sugar, cornstarch, and salt. Whisk in the water, orange zest and juice, then whisk in the egg yolks. Bring to a boil over medium heat, stirring constantly. Boil, stirring, for 1 minute. Remove from the heat, add the butter, and stir until melted. Pour the hot filling into the pie shell.

5. Make the meringue topping. In a large heatproof bowl, whisk together the egg whites and sugar. Set the bowl over a saucepan of simmering water and whisk for 2 to 3 minutes, until the sugar has completely dissolved. Remove from the saucepan and whisk in the salt. Using an electric mixer, beat the whites at medium-high speed until stiff peaks form.

6. Spoon dollops of the meringue onto the filling. With a rubber spatula, spread the meringue evenly over the filling, making sure to touch the edges of the pie shell. Use the back of a large metal spoon to create decorative peaks of meringue.

7. Bake the pie for 10 to 12 minutes, until the meringue is a light golden brown. Let the pie cool completely on a wire rack. Serve at room temperature or refrigerate, uncovered, for up to 1 day and serve chilled.

SERVES 8

key lime pie

T HE AUTHENTIC VERSION OF THIS CLASSIC pie is made with the sweet, small yellow-green Key limes from Florida. However, it's quite delicious made with regular supermarket limes, and, in fact, many people prefer their flavor. A graham cracker crust is traditional, while the topping is sometimes meringue and sometimes whipped cream, as it is here.

GRAHAM CRACKER CRUST

1 package (11 full sheets) graham crackers, finely crushed

2 1/2 tablespoons sugar

5 tablespoons unsalted butter, melted

KEY LIME FILLING

4 large egg yolks

1 (14-ounce) can sweetened condensed milk

2 teaspoons grated lime zest

1/2 cup fresh lime juice (from 3 or 4 limes)

WHIPPED CREAM TOPPING

1 cup heavy cream

1 tablespoon sugar

1/2 teaspoon vanilla extract

1. Preheat the oven to 350°F.

2. Make the graham cracker crust. In a medium bowl, combine the graham cracker crumbs and sugar. Add the melted butter and stir until the crumbs are evenly moistened. Using your fingertips, press the crumb mixture evenly over the bottom and up the sides of a 9-inch pie plate.

3. Bake the crust for 8 to 10 minutes, until the edges are light golden brown. Let the crust cool to room temperature on a wire rack. Reduce the oven temperature to 325°F.

4. Make the Key lime filling. In a large bowl, whisk the egg yolks until blended. Whisk in the condensed milk, then whisk in the lime zest and juice until blended. (If necessary, set the filling aside briefly at room temperature until the crust has cooled.) Pour the filling into the crust.

5. Bake the pie for 15 to 17 minutes, until the filling is just set; the center should jiggle slightly if gently shaken. Let the pie cool completely on a wire rack. Refrigerate the pie for 3 to 4 hours, until chilled.

6. Shortly before serving, make the whipped cream topping. In a large bowl, combine the cream, sugar, and vanilla and beat with an electric mixer until stiff peaks form. Spread the whipped cream evenly over the top of the pie. (For a fancier touch, transfer the whipped cream to a pastry bag fitted with a large star tip and pipe a border of rosettes around the edge of the pie.) Serve immediately, or refrigerate for up to 1 hour.

SERVES 8

shaker *lemon pie*

SEEDLESS, TART LEMONS ARE THINLY SLICED AND suspended in a creamy lemon curd in this old-fashioned pie. You'll find seedless lemons in specialty food shops—not having to remove seeds makes it worth the trip! Start this recipe a day before you want to serve the pie, so you have time to soak the lemon slices in their sugared juice. For a pretty garnish, cut the dough scraps into small lemon shapes, brush the underside with a small amount of water, and arrange them on the crust before sprinkling with sugar and baking.

> **2 large seedless lemons, well washed**
>
> **2 cups sugar, plus 1 tablespoon for sprinkling**
>
> **1 recipe Flaky Pie Pastry (p. 37)**
>
> **4 large eggs**
>
> **1 tablespoon milk**

1. Trim off the ends of the lemons and cut each in half lengthwise. Cut the halves crosswise in very thin slices, about 1/8 inch thick.

2. In a medium bowl, stir together the lemon slices, any accumulated juices, and 2 cups sugar. Cover with plastic wrap and set aside, at room temperature, for 24 hours.

3. Position a rack in the lower third of the oven; preheat the oven to 450°F.

4. On a lightly floured surface, roll out one of the dough disks to a 12 1/2-inch round. Fit the dough into a 9-inch pie plate.

Trim the edge of the dough, leaving a 1/2-inch overhang. Fold the excess dough under itself and crimp the edge. Refrigerate for 30 minutes.

5. On a lightly floured surface, roll out the remaining dough to a 10-inch round.

6. In a small bowl, beat the eggs until they are well mixed. Stir them into the lemon mixture until well combined. Spoon the mixture into the pie crust. Cover with the top crust and trim and crimp the edge. Brush the surface of the crust with the milk. Using a small sharp knife, cut four steam vents in the top of the crust. Sprinkle with the remaining 1 tablespoon sugar.

7. Bake the pie for 20 minutes. Reduce the heat to 350°F and bake for 25 to 30 minutes more, until a thin knife inserted into one of the slashes comes out fairly clean and the crust is golden. Let the pie cool on a wire rack for at least 2 hours before serving.

SERVES 8

banana butterscotch
cream pie

G OLDEN BUTTERSCOTCH PUDDING, WHIPPED cream, and ripe bananas make up the filling of this childhood favorite.

BUTTERSCOTCH FILLING

3 cups milk

4 large egg yolks

3/4 cup packed brown sugar

1/4 cup cornstarch

2 tablespoons unsalted butter

2 teaspoons vanilla extract

1/2 recipe Flaky Pie Pastry (p. 37)

1 cup heavy cream

2 ripe bananas

Chocolate shavings, for garnish

1. Make the butterscotch filling. In a large heavy saucepan, scald 2 1/2 cups of milk over medium heat.

2. Meanwhile, in a mixing bowl, whisk together the remaining milk, egg yolks, brown sugar, and cornstarch until smooth.

3. Pour about 1 cup of the hot milk into the egg yolk mixture and whisk vigorously. Pour the warmed yolk mixture into the saucepan of hot milk and bring to a simmer, whisking, for 2 minutes. Remove the pan from the heat and whisk in the butter and vanilla. Strain the pudding into a clean bowl. Cover with a piece of plastic wrap directly on the surface to prevent a skin from forming and refrigerate for 2 to 3 hours.

4. On a lightly floured surface, roll out the dough to a 12 1/2-inch round. Fit the dough into a 9-inch pie plate. Trim the overhanging dough even with the edge of the pie plate and crimp the edge. Refrigerate.

5. Preheat the oven to 375°F.

6. Line the pie shell with foil and fill with dried beans or rice. Bake for 15 minutes. Remove the foil and beans and bake the shell for 8 to 10 minutes longer, until golden brown. Let the pie shell cool completely on a wire rack.

7. In a medium bowl, beat the cream with an electric mixer until stiff peaks form.

8. Peel and slice the bananas. Lay the slices on the bottom of the pie crust, then top with the pudding. Using a pastry bag with a medium star tip, pipe the whipped cream decoratively over the pie. Sprinkle the chocolate shavings on the cream and serve the pie immediately.

SERVES 8

rich chocolate
cream pie

ICH, CREAMY, AND DEEPLY CHOCOLATY, this pie needs no adornment. If you do choose to gild the lily, decorate the top with rosettes of whipped cream, using a pastry bag fitted with a large star tip.

1/2 recipe **Flaky Pie Pastry (p. 37)**

RICH CHOCOLATE FILLING

2 cups milk

2/3 cup heavy cream

1 cup sugar

4 large egg yolks

3 tablespoons cornstarch

Pinch of salt

8 ounces bittersweet or semisweet chocolate,
finely chopped

2 teaspoons vanilla extract

1. On a lightly floured surface, roll out the dough to a 12 1/2-inch round. Fit the dough into a 9-inch pie plate. Trim the edges of the dough, leaving a 1/2-inch overhang. Fold the excess dough under itself and crimp the edges. Refrigerate for 30 minutes.

2. Preheat the oven to 375°F.

3. Line the pie shell with foil and fill with dried beans or rice. Bake for 15 minutes. Remove the foil and beans and bake the shell for 8 to 10 minutes longer, until golden brown. Let the pie shell cool completely on a wire rack.

4. Make the rich chocolate filling. In a large heavy saucepan, combine all but 2 tablespoons of the milk with the cream and sugar. Bring the mixture to a boil over medium heat, stirring to dissolve the sugar.

5. Meanwhile, in a large bowl, combine the egg yolks, cornstarch, salt, and the remaining 2 tablespoons milk and whisk until smooth.

6. Whisking constantly, gradually pour about half of the hot milk into the egg yolk mixture. Pour the warmed yolk mixture into the saucepan of hot milk and bring to a very gentle boil over medium-low heat, whisking constantly. Boil, whisking, for 1 minute. Remove from the heat and whisk in the chocolate until it is completely melted. Transfer the filling to a bowl and whisk in the vanilla. Cover with a piece of plastic wrap directly touching the surface to prevent a skin from forming and let cool to room temperature.

7. Pour the cooled filling into the pie shell and smooth the top with a rubber spatula. Cover loosely and refrigerate for at least 2 hours, until chilled, before serving. Refrigerate any leftovers, covered with plastic wrap.

SERVES 8

coconut cream *pie*

DELICATE TEXTURE AND LOTS OF COCONUT make this pie miles above your average coffee-shop version.

1/2 recipe Flaky Pie Pastry (p. 37)

COCONUT CREAM FILLING
2 cups milk
2/3 cup heavy cream
3/4 cup sugar
I large egg
2 large egg yolks
3 tablespoons cornstarch
Pinch of salt
I tablespoon unsalted butter, cut in pieces
I 1/2 teaspoons vanilla extract
I 1/4 cups sweetened shredded coconut

WHIPPED CREAM TOPPING
I cup heavy cream
I tablespoon sugar
1/2 teaspoon vanilla extract

**1/3 cup sweetened shredded coconut, toasted,
 for garnish**

1. On a lightly floured surface, roll out the dough to a 12 1/2-inch round. Fit into a 9-inch pie plate. Trim the edges of the dough leaving a 1/2 inch overhang. Fold the excess dough under itself and crimp the edge. Refrigerate for 30 minutes.

2. Preheat the oven to 375°F.

3. Line the pie shell with foil and fill with dried beans or rice. Bake for 15 minutes. Remove the foil and beans and bake for 8 to 10 minutes longer, until golden brown. Let the pie shell cool completely on a wire rack.

4. Make the coconut cream filling. In a large heavy saucepan, combine all but 2 tablespoons of the milk with the cream and sugar and bring to a boil, stirring to dissolve the sugar.

5. Meanwhile, in a large bowl, whisk the egg, egg yolks, cornstarch, salt, and the remaining milk until smooth.

6. Whisking constantly, gradually pour about half of the hot milk into the egg yolk mixture. Pour the warmed yolk mixture into the saucepan of hot milk and bring to a very gentle boil over medium-low heat, whisking constantly. Boil gently, whisking, for 1 minute. Remove from the heat and whisk in the butter and vanilla until the butter is melted. Stir in the coconut. Cover with a piece of plastic wrap directly touching the surface and let cool completely.

7. Pour the cooled filling into the pie shell and smooth the top. Cover loosely and refrigerate for at least 2 hours, until chilled.

8. Shortly before serving, make the whipped cream topping. In a large bowl, combine the cream, sugar, and vanilla and beat with an electric mixer until stiff peaks form. Spread the whipped cream evenly over the top of the pie and sprinkle the toasted coconut on top. Serve immediately, or refrigerate for up to 1 hour before serving.

SERVES 8

souffléd sweet *potato pie*

THE CLOUD-LIKE FILLING OF THIS LIGHTER-than-average sweet potato pie is studded with jewel-like golden raisins and given a warm and wonderfully rich accent from the rum.

1/2 recipe **Flaky Pie Pastry (p. 37)**

1 1/2 cups **mashed cooked sweet potato**

1 1/2 cups **milk**

1/2 cup plus 2 tablespoons **sugar**

4 large **egg yolks**

1/4 cup **golden raisins**

2 tablespoons **rum**

1 teaspoon **vanilla extract**

1/2 teaspoon **freshly grated nutmeg**

Pinch of salt

3 large **egg whites**

1. On a lightly floured surface, roll out the dough to a 12 1/2-inch round. Fit the dough into a 9-inch pie plate. Trim the overhanging dough even with the edge of the pie plate and crimp the edge. Refrigerate.

2. Preheat the oven to 325°F.

3. Line the pie shell with foil and fill with dried beans or rice. Bake for 15 minutes. Remove the foil and beans and bake for 8 to 10 minutes longer, until golden brown. Let the pie shell cool completely on a wire rack.

4. In a large bowl, mix together the sweet potato, milk, 1/2 cup of the sugar, the egg yolks, raisins, rum, vanilla, nutmeg, and salt.

5. In a large bowl, beat the egg whites with an electric mixer on medium speed until frothy. Gradually add the remaining 2 tablespoons sugar and increase the speed to high. Beat until stiff peaks form.

6. Gently fold the beaten whites into the sweet potato mixture until uniform in color. Pour the mixture into the pie shell and smooth the top with a rubber spatula.

7. Bake the pie for 25 minutes, or until the filling is puffed and set. Let the pie cool on a wire rack. Serve warm or at room temperature.

SERVES 8

southern pecan *pie*

BOURBON AND PECANS ARE A NATURAL southern combination. Just a tablespoon of the whiskey adds a subtle flavor and cuts the sweetness that often overwhelms pecan pie.

1/2 recipe **Flaky Pie Pastry (p. 37)**

BOURBON-PECAN FILLING

3 large eggs

3/4 cup granulated sugar

1/4 cup packed light brown sugar

1 cup light corn syrup

1 tablespoon unsalted butter, melted

1 1/2 teaspoons vanilla extract

1/8 teaspoon salt

1 tablespoon bourbon (optional)

1 1/2 cups pecan halves

1. Position a rack in the lower third of the oven; preheat the oven to 350°F.

2. On a lightly floured surface, roll out the dough to a 12 1/2-inch round. Fit it into a 9-inch glass pie plate. Trim the edges of the dough, leaving a 1/2-inch overhang. Fold the excess dough under itself and crimp the edge. Refrigerate.

3. Make the bourbon-pecan filling. In a large bowl, beat the eggs with an electric mixer until frothy. Beat in the granulated and brown sugars. Add the corn syrup, melted butter, vanilla, and salt and beat until smooth. Beat in the bourbon, if using. Stir in the pecans. Pour the filling into the pie shell.

4. Bake the pie for 45 to 50 minutes, until the filling is puffed up and just set in the center. Let the pie cool completely on a wire rack. Serve at room temperature, or refrigerate and serve chilled.

SERVES 8

lemon chess *pie*

hERE'S A FAVORITE SOUTHERN DESSERT. Although the filling in this version is somewhat lighter than usual, it is still rich, with the sweetness of the custard balanced by the tartness of the lemon. It's best served at room temperature the day it's made, but it can be refrigerated and served cold.

1/2 recipe **Flaky Pie Pastry (p. 37)**

LEMON FILLING

1 1/2 cups sugar

3 large eggs

1 tablespoon all-purpose flour

Pinch of salt

6 tablespoons (3/4 stick) unsalted butter,
   melted and cooled

1 1/2 teaspoons grated lemon zest

2 tablespoons fresh lemon juice

1. Position a rack in the lower third of the oven; preheat the oven to 350°F.

2. On a lightly floured surface, roll out the dough to a 12 1/2-inch round. Fit it into a 9-inch glass pie plate. Trim the edges of the dough, leaving a 1/2-inch overhang. Fold the excess dough under itself and crimp the edges. Refrigerate.

3. Make the lemon filling. In a large bowl, beat the sugar and eggs until well blended. Beat in the flour and salt. Add the melted butter, lemon zest, and lemon juice, beating to mix well. Pour the filling into the pie shell.

4. Bake the pie for 40 to 45 minutes, until the top is golden brown (a thin crust will form) and the filling is set. Let the pie cool completely on a wire rack. Serve at room temperature, or refrigerate and serve chilled.

SERVES 8 TO 10

raspberry brown *butter tart*

OTHER BERRIES, SUCH AS BLACKBERRIES OR blueberries, or even pitted cherries, would also be good in this easy-to-make recipe. The brown butter gives the unusual and delicious sweet filling a hint of nuttiness. If you dare indulge, try it topped with a touch of whipped cream.

1 sheet frozen puff pastry (half a 1 7 1/4-ounce
    package), thawed according to package directions
11 tablespoons unsalted butter
3 large eggs
1 cup granulated sugar
3 1/2 tablespoons all-purpose flour
1 1/2 teaspoons vanilla extract
1 cup fresh raspberries
Confectioners' sugar, for dusting (optional)

1. Position a rack in the lower third of the oven; preheat the oven to 350°F.

2. Unfold the pastry on a lightly floured surface and roll it out to a rough 12-inch square. Fit it into a 9-inch fluted tart pan with a removable bottom. Trim the dough even with the top of the pan. Refrigerate while you proceed.

3. In a small heavy saucepan, melt the butter over high heat, then cook for 8 to 10 minutes, until it is golden brown and has a nutty aroma.

4. Meanwhile, in a medium bowl, whisk the eggs and granulated sugar until well blended. Whisk in the flour.

5. Gradually whisk the browned butter into the egg mixture. Whisk in the vanilla until combined.

6. Scatter the raspberries evenly over the bottom of the tart shell. Slowly pour the filling evenly over the berries.

7. Bake the tart for 45 to 50 minutes, until the top is golden brown and the filling is set. (It's fine if there are a few cracks in the top of the tart.) Let the tart cool completely on a wire rack. Serve at room temperature, or refrigerate and serve chilled.

8. Just before serving, dust the top of the tart generously with confectioners' sugar, if desired.

SERVES 6 TO 8

pear tart with *almond cream*

HERE ARE FEW DESSERTS AS SATISFYING OR elegant as this combination of soft, ripe pears, crisp tart pastry, and sweet almond cream. The traditional cream, once a chore to make by hand, is easily whipped up in a food processor. Because of the richness of the filling, serve this tart with a just few berries, such as raspberries or blackberries, and a sprig of mint for garnish.

HOMEY PIES & ELEGANT TARTS

1 recipe Sweet Tart Crust (p. 37)

5 tablespoons sugar

1/4 cup whole blanched almonds

3/4 cup heavy cream

1 large egg

1 teaspoon vanilla extract

1/8 teaspoon almond extract

Pinch of salt

6 medium pears

1. Preheat the oven to 375°F.

2. On a lightly floured surface, roll out the tart crust to an 11-inch round. Fit the dough into a 9-inch tart pan with a removable bottom, folding the extra dough back over the inner sides of the tart to strengthen them. Prick the dough all over with the tines of a fork. Line the shell with foil and fill with dried beans or rice.

3. Bake the tart shell for 15 minutes, then remove the foil and beans and bake for 10 to 15 minutes longer, until golden brown. Let the tart shell cool completely on a wire rack.

4. In a food processor, process the sugar and almonds until the almonds are finely ground. Add the cream, egg, vanilla, almond extract, and salt and process until smooth.

5. Peel, core and slice the pears lengthwise into eighths. Place the pear slices in an overlapping circular pattern over the bottom of the tart shell. Carefully pour the almond cream on top, spreading it with a rubber spatula to cover the pears evenly.

6. Bake the tart for 45 minutes, or until the pears are tender and the almond cream is set. Let the tart cool on a wire rack. Serve warm or at room temperature.

SERVES 8

lemon–cream cheese *tartlets*

tHESE INDIVIDUAL TARTS ARE PERFECT FOR a formal dinner party. Serve them on their own, or decorate them with a few berries. For an elegant look, garnish each one with a strip of candied lemon peel. You will need six four-inch tartlet pans.

1 recipe Sweet Tart Crust (p. 37)

LEMON–CREAM CHEESE FILLING
4 ounces cream cheese, at room temperature
1/2 cup plus 1 tablespoon superfine sugar (see Note)
2 teaspoons grated lemon zest
1 1/2 tablespoons fresh lemon juice
1/2 cup heavy cream

1. Divide the dough into 6 pieces and shape each one into a disk. On a floured surface, roll out each piece of dough to a 6-inch round. Fit each round into a 4-inch fluted tart pan with a removable bottom and trim the excess dough even with the edge of the pan. Place the 6 tartlet pans on a baking sheet and refrigerate for 30 minutes.

2. Preheat the oven to 375°F.

3. Line each tart shell with foil and fill with dried beans or rice. Bake, still on the baking sheet, for 15 minutes. Remove the foil and beans and bake for 8 to 10 minutes longer, until the pastry is golden brown. Transfer the baking sheet to a wire rack and let the pastry cool completely.

4. Make the lemon–cream cheese filling. In a large bowl, beat the cream cheese with an electric mixer until light and fluffy. Add the sugar, lemon zest, and lemon juice and beat until light and fluffy.

5. In a medium bowl, beat the cream (no need to wash the beaters) until it forms soft peaks. Using a rubber spatula, fold a few spoonfuls of the whipped cream into the cream cheese mixture to lighten it, then fold in the remaining cream.

6. Unmold the tartlet shells. Spoon the filling into the tartlet shells. Serve immediately, or refrigerate for up to 6 hours before serving.

SERVES 6

NOTE: If you don't have superfine sugar, you can make your own by processing granulated sugar in the food processor for a minute or two, until fine.

chocolate-raspberry *tartlets*

T HE CHOCOLATE-CREAM FILLING IN THESE tartlets is a mixture known as ganache, which is also used to make truffles. Here it is briefly whipped to give it a meltingly smooth texture. You could use small strawberries or even blackberries rather than the raspberries in these rich, dark chocolate tartlets; choose whatever is in season.

1 recipe Sweet Tart Crust (p. 37)

DARK CHOCOLATE FILLING
**4 ounces bittersweet or semisweet chocolate,
     finely chopped**
3/4 cup heavy cream
**1 1/2 teaspoons Chambord (black raspberry liqueur;
     optional)**

Generous 1 1/2 cups raspberries

1. Divide the dough into 6 pieces and shape each one into a disk. On a lightly floured surface, roll out each piece of dough to a 6-inch round. Fit each round into a 4-inch fluted tart pan with a removable bottom. Trim the excess dough even with the edge of the pan. Place the 6 tartlet pans on a baking sheet and refrigerate for 30 minutes.

2. Preheat the oven to 375°F.

3. Line each tartlet shell with foil and fill with dried beans or rice. Bake, still on the baking sheet, for 15 minutes. Remove the foil and beans and bake for 8 to 10 minutes longer,

until the pastry is golden brown. Transfer the baking sheet to a wire rack and let cool completely.

4. Meanwhile, make the dark chocolate filling. Place the chocolate in a medium bowl. In a small saucepan, bring the cream just to a boil. Pour the cream over the chocolate and let stand for 30 seconds. Gently whisk until the chocolate is completely melted and smooth. Stir in the Chambord, if using. Let cool to room temperature, then refrigerate, stirring occasionally, for about 1 1/2 hours, until very cold but not set.

5. Beat the chilled filling, using an electric mixer on low speed, just until it begins to form stiff peaks; do not overbeat.

6. Unmold the tartlet shells. Spoon the filling into the tartlet shells and smooth the top with the back of a small spoon. Arrange the raspberries in concentric rings on top of the filling, starting at the edge of each tartlet and working toward the center. Serve immediately, or refrigerate for up to 6 hours. Remove from the refrigerator about 30 minutes before serving.

SERVES 6

plum almond *galette*

a GALETTE IS A FLAT FREE-FORM TART originally from France. It can have many different fillings, both savory and sweet. This golden-crusted tart is put together in minutes, but it looks and tastes as if you spent all day. If plums are not available, try peaches or nectarines.

I sheet frozen puff pastry (half a 17 1/4-ounce package), thawed according to package directions

2 cups pitted and sliced plums

I large egg, beaten

1/3 cup sugar

1/3 cup sliced blanched almonds

1/4 teaspoon almond extract

2 tablespoons milk

1. Preheat the oven to 375°F.

2. Unfold the puff pastry and place it on an ungreased baking sheet. Refrigerate while you proceed.

3. In a medium bowl, mix together the plums, egg, sugar, almonds, and almond extract until well combined. Spoon the plum mixture onto the puff pastry, leaving a 1-inch border around the sides. Fold the sides of the pastry over the filling to partially enclose it. Using a pastry brush, coat the top of the pastry with the milk.

4. Bake the galette for 35 minutes, or until the crust is golden brown and the filling is bubbling. Let the galette cool slightly on a wire rack. Serve warm or at room temperature.

SERVES 6 TO 8

Chapter Four
heavenly cakes

Cake Tips

A birthday wouldn't be a birthday without a cake. Cakes are always appropriate for any celebration, whether an anniversary, bridal shower, or family reunion. Following are tips to get you on the way to success.

- Start with the right size pan. If the pan is too small, the batter may overflow; if the pan is too large, you will have thinner layers than you want, and they may be tough. In either case, the baking time will be off.

- For most cakes, the pan or pans must be greased and, often, floured as well. (The pans for angel food cakes are never greased, because the slippery sides would prevent the batter from climbing up to its impressive height.) You can use softened butter or margarine or vegetable shortening to grease cake pans. With your fingertips or a piece of paper towel, rub the butter generously and evenly over the bottom and sides of the pan, making sure to get into the corners. To flour the pan, sprinkle a tablespoon or so of flour into the pan and tilt and turn the pan so that the bottom and sides are evenly coated. Shake out the excess flour. Occasionally a cake pan must be lined with waxed paper or parchment paper to ensure that the cake can be unmolded successfully. Cut a piece of paper that just fits in the bottom of the pan, grease the pan (this will anchor the paper in place), and then grease the paper; flour the paper and sides of the pan with flour if called for.

- To test the doneness of most cakes, insert a toothpick into the center of the cake and remove it; if it comes out clean, the cake is done. For some recipes, however, the cake is done when the toothpick comes out almost clean or with a few moist crumbs clinging to it. For tall cakes, like angel food, a toothpick will not be long enough—use a metal cake tester instead.

- To unmold a cake, run a thin sharp knife around the side of the pan (be careful not to cut into the cake), then invert the cake onto another wire rack.

- Before frosting a cake, make sure the cake is completely cool, or the frosting may melt. To anchor the cake to the plate and prevent slipping, place a small dab of frosting in the center of the plate before placing the first layer, or the cake, on it.

- To frost a layer cake, first brush away any loose crumbs. Spread an even layer of frosting over the first cake layer with an icing spatula; if the frosting is soft, don't spread it all the way to the edges of the cake,the weight of the top layer will do that for you. Top with the second layer, centering it over the bottom layer. Then frost the top and side of the cake. Use the back of a metal spoon to make swirls in the frosting on top of the cake if you like. For a smooth finish, run the icing spatula around the sides of the cake.

- Most butter cake layers can be made ahead and frozen, well wrapped in plastic wrap and then foil, for up to 2 months. Then, when the occasion arises, you can just thaw the layers, frost them, and serve. Most loaf cakes and other plain cakes also freeze well.

chocolate *frosting*

USE THIS SIMPLE VERSATILE FROSTING FOR any of your favorite cakes. Don't overwhisk when you combine the cream and chocolate, but do make sure the chocolate is completely melted and smooth. The frosting thickens to the desired consistency as it cools, so make it before you make the cake layers. For an even richer, darker chocolate frosting, use a good-quality bittersweet chocolate, such as Callebaut or Lindt, instead of semisweet.

9 ounces semisweet chocolate, finely chopped

1 1/3 cups heavy cream

1 1/2 tablespoons unsalted butter, cut in
  1/2-inch pieces

1 teaspoon vanilla extract

1. Place the chocolate in a medium bowl. In a small saucepan, bring the cream and butter just to a boil, stirring occasionally until the butter has melted. Pour the hot cream mixture over the chocolate and let stand for 30 seconds. Gently whisk until the chocolate is melted and well incorporated. Stir in the vanilla.

2. Let cool, then cover and refrigerate, stirring occasionally, for about 2 hours, until thickened and spreadable.

MAKES ABOUT 2 1/4 CUPS

sour cream *fudge frosting*

OUR CREAM GIVES THIS RICH FROSTING a delightful subtle tang that adults will appreciate; children may prefer the Chocolate Frosting (left).

10 ounces bittersweet or semisweet chocolate,
  coarsely chopped

1 1/3 cups sour cream

1 teaspoon vanilla extract

1. In the top of a double boiler over barely simmering water, melt the chocolate, stirring occasionally, until smooth. Remove from the heat.

2. Meanwhile, in a large bowl, combine the sour cream and vanilla and blend well.

3. Using an electric mixer on low speed, gradually beat the warm chocolate into the sour cream, then beat just until smooth and shiny. Let stand at room temperature, stirring once or twice, for about 30 minutes, until cool and slightly thickened.

MAKES ABOUT 2 1/4 CUPS

seven-minute *icing*

easy buttercream *frosting*

tHIS CLASSIC FLUFFY, PURE WHITE CAKE frosting is made by cooking and beating egg whites and sugar. The recipe makes enough icing to fill and frost a three-layer cake generously. The icing should be used as soon as it is made.

2 1/4 cups sugar

3/8 teaspoon cream of tartar

3 large egg whites

7 1/2 tablespoons cold water

2 1/4 teaspoons light corn syrup

3/4 teaspoon vanilla extract

1. In a large, deep, heatproof bowl, combine the sugar, cream of tarter, egg whites, water, and corn syrup, and beat with an electric mixer on low speed until well blended.

2. Set the bowl over a pot of simmering water (the bottom of the bowl should not touch the water) and beat on medium speed, scraping down the side of the bowl 2 or 3 times, for 3 minutes. Increase the speed to high and beat for 4 minutes, or until the icing is thick and shiny and forms soft peaks.

3. Remove the bowl from the heat and beat in the vanilla. Beat for about 30 seconds longer, or until the icing again forms soft peaks. Use immediately.

VARIATIONS

Seven-Minute Coconut Icing: After adding the vanilla, using a rubber spatula, fold 1/2 cup sweetened shredded coconut into the frosting.

MAKES ABOUT 5 CUPS

tHIS SIMPLE, QUICKLY MADE FROSTING IS perfect for decorating all kinds of cakes and cupcakes, or for sandwiching in between two cookies.

1/2 cup (1 stick) unsalted butter,

at room temperature

3 cups confectioners' sugar

2 tablespoons milk

1 teaspoon vanilla extract

Pinch of salt

1. In a large bowl, cream the butter with an electric mixer until very soft and light, about 3 minutes. Add the remaining ingredients and beat until smooth and fluffy. Use immediately, or cover and refrigerate until needed.

MAKES ABOUT 4 CUPS

glazed lemon-scented *pound cake*

SOUR CREAM GIVES THIS CAKE A LUSCIOUS, almost creamy, texture. The simple lemon glaze intensifies the flavor of the lemon cake and turns a simple loaf cake into something special.

LEMON-SCENTED POUND CAKE

2 cups all-purpose flour

1 teaspoon baking powder

1/2 teaspoon baking soda

1/4 teaspoon salt

1/2 cup (1 stick) unsalted butter,
    at room temperature

1 1/4 cups granulated sugar

2 large eggs, at room temperature

1 1/2 tablespoons lemon extract

2 teaspoons grated lemon zest

1 (8-ounce) container sour cream

LEMON GLAZE

1/2 cup confectioners' sugar

1 1/2 teaspoons fresh lemon juice

1 to 2 teaspoons cream or milk

1. Make the lemon-scented pound cake. Preheat the oven to 350°F. Grease and flour a 9- x 5-inch loaf pan.

2. In a medium bowl, whisk together the flour, baking powder, baking soda, and salt. Set aside.

3. In a large bowl, beat the butter and granulated sugar with an electric mixer until light and fluffy. Add the eggs one at a time, beating well after each addition. Beat in the lemon extract and zest. On low speed, add the flour mixture alternating with the sour cream, beginning and ending with the flour mixture. Pour the batter into the prepared pan and smooth the top.

4. Bake the cake for 50 to 55 minutes, until a toothpick inserted into the center comes out clean. Let cool in the pan on a wire rack for 10 minutes. Remove the cake from the pan, set right side up on the rack, and let cool completely.

5. Make the lemon glaze. In a small bowl, combine the confectioners' sugar, lemon juice, and just enough cream to make a smooth glaze.

6. Drizzle the glaze slowly over the top of the cake. Transfer the cake to a serving platter and let the glaze set before serving.

SERVES 8 TO 10

heavenly coconut *cake*

THREE LAYERS HIGH, FROSTED WITH GLOSSY white icing and finished with an extravagant amount of coconut, this is truly a stunning cake for a special occasion. If you have a standing electric mixer, you'll want to use it for this recipe.

HEAVENLY CAKES

3 cups all-purpose flour

1 tablespoon baking powder

1/2 teaspoon salt

14 tablespoons (1 3/4 sticks) unsalted butter, at room temperature

2 cups sugar

4 large eggs, at room temperature

1 large egg yolk, at room temperature

2 teaspoons vanilla extract

1 1/3 cups milk

1 recipe Seven-Minute Coconut Icing (p. 70)

1 1/2 cups sweetened shredded coconut

1. Preheat the oven to 350°F. Grease and flour three 9-inch round cake pans.

2. In a large bowl, whisk together the flour, baking powder, and salt. In another large bowl, beat the butter and sugar with an electric mixer until light and fluffy. Add the eggs and egg yolk one at a time, beating well after each addition. Beat in the vanilla. On low speed, beat in the flour mixture in 3 additions, alternating with the milk, beginning and ending with the flour mixture. Pour the batter into the prepared pans and smooth the tops.

3. Bake the cakes for 25 to 27 minutes, until a toothpick inserted into the center comes out clean. Let cool in the pans on wire racks for 10 minutes. Remove the layers from the pans, set right side up on the racks, and let cool completely.

4. Place one of the cake layers on a serving plate and spread a generous layer of icing over the top. Place the second layer on top and spread with generous layer of icing. Place the third layer on top and frost the top and side of the cake with the remaining icing. Scatter about 1/2 cup of the coconut evenly over the top of the cake, and press the remaining coconut into the side. The cake can be made several hours ahead and set aside at cool room temperature.

SERVES 12 TO 14

rich vanilla
pound cake

C AKE FLOUR LIGHTENS THE TEXTURE OF THIS deliciously buttery pound cake. Serve it as is or topped with fruit and ice cream. Once you have scraped the seeds out of the vanilla pod, don't throw out the pod. Bury it in your sugar canister, it will add a delicate flavor to the sugar.

> **I vanilla bean, sliced lengthwise**
>
> **2 1/2 cups cake flour (not self-rising)**
>
> **I teaspoon baking powder**
>
> **1/2 teaspoon salt**
>
> **I cup (2 sticks) unsalted butter,**
>   **at room temperature**
>
> **I 3/4 cups sugar**
>
> **5 large eggs**
>
> **I tablespoon vanilla extract**
>
> **1/4 cup milk**

1. Preheat the oven to 325°F. Grease a 10-cup Bundt pan.

2. Using the tip of a small sharp knife, scrape the seeds out of the vanilla bean. Reserve the seeds. In a medium bowl, combine the flour, baking powder, and salt with a whisk. Set aside.

3. In another medium bowl, beat the butter with an electric mixer until creamy. Add the sugar and continue to beat for 2 minutes, or until the mixture is light and fluffy. Beat in the eggs, one at a time, beating for 30 to 40 seconds after each addition. Scrape down the bowl frequently with a rubber spatula. Blend in the vanilla and reserved vanilla seeds.

4. On low speed, add the flour mixture alternating with the milk, beginning and ending with the flour mixture. Pour the batter into the prepared pan and smooth the top.

5. Bake the cake for 60 minutes, or until a cake tester inserted into the center comes out clean. Let cool in the pan on a wire rack for 10 minutes. Remove the cake from the pan and let cool completely.

SERVES 12 TO 14

QUEEN OF THE KITCHEN TIP

Turning Cakes into Cupcakes

Almost any cake recipe can be used to make cupcakes. Fill muffin cups lined with paper liners about two-thirds full with the batter. Bake at the temperature indicated in the cake recipe, but reduce the baking time. Most cupcakes will take 15 to 20 minutes; start checking after 15 minutes, and then check every 2 or 3 minutes until a toothpick inserted in the center of one cupcake comes out clean. Let cool in the pan on a rack. For a children's birthday party, let each child decorate his or her own cupcake, see page 84 (Devil's Food Cupcakes) for some ideas.

apple spice cake with *caramel glaze*

HE TRADITIONAL AUTUMNAL COMBINATION of caramel and apples is spiced up with cinnamon, allspice, and nutmeg in this moist and tender cake. This recipe is quick and easy if you use a food processor to chop the nuts and apples.

APPLE SPICE CAKE

3 cups all-purpose flour

1 teaspoon baking soda

1/2 teaspoon ground cinnamon

1/4 teaspoon ground allspice

1/4 teaspoon freshly grated nutmeg

1 teaspoon salt

1 1/2 cups granulated sugar

1/2 cup packed dark brown sugar

1 1/2 cups vegetable oil

3 large eggs, at room temperature

2 teaspoons vanilla extract

3 cups chopped Granny Smith apples
    (from about 2 1/2 apples)

2 cups walnut halves, coarsely chopped

CARAMEL GLAZE

1/2 cup packed dark brown sugar

1/4 cup (1/2 stick) unsalted butter

1/4 cup heavy cream

1. Make the apple spice cake. Preheat the oven to 325°F. Grease and flour a 10-inch Bundt pan.

2. In a medium bowl, whisk together the flour, baking soda, cinnamon, allspice, nutmeg, and salt. Set aside.

3. In a large bowl, preferably the bowl of a standing electric mixer, beat together the granulated and brown sugars and the oil until smooth. Add the eggs one at a time, beating well after each addition and scraping down the bowl with a rubber spatula. Beat in the vanilla. On low speed, add the flour mixture in 3 additions. Using a large wooden spoon, stir in the apples and walnuts. Pour the batter into the prepared pan and smooth the top.

4. Bake the cake for 65 to 70 minutes, until a cake tester inserted into the center comes out clean. Let cool for 10 minutes, then remove the cake from the pan and let cool completely.

5. Make the caramel glaze. In a small heavy saucepan, combine the brown sugar, butter, and cream. Bring to a boil, stirring to dissolve the sugar. Boil, stirring occasionally, for 3 minutes, or until slightly thickened. Remove from the heat and let cool for 10 minutes, or until the glaze thickens slightly but is still pourable.

6. Set the cake, still on the wire rack, on a baking sheet. Drizzle the glaze slowly over the top, letting some of it run down the side. Transfer the cake to a serving plate and let the glaze set before serving.

SERVES 12

lemon pudding *cake*

UDDING AND CAKE IN ONE! WHEN BAKED AND cooled, this ever-so-simple batter magically separates into a light lemony sponge cake on top of buttery lemon curd.

1/4 cup (1/2 stick) unsalted butter, melted

3 lemons

1 1/2 cups plain yogurt

1 1/4 cups sugar

3 large eggs

1/4 cup all-purpose flour

1. Preheat the oven to 325°F. Grease a 1-quart casserole.

2. Using a grater, grate the zest of 1 lemon. In a food processor, mix the melted butter and lemon zest until combined.

3. Squeeze the juice from the 3 lemons and strain into the butter mixture. Add the yogurt, sugar, eggs, and flour and process for 3 minutes.

4. Pour the batter into the prepared casserole and bake for 50 minutes, or until lightly golden around the edges and springs back when touched. Transfer the casserole to a wire rack and let the cake cool slightly. Serve warm.

SERVES 4 TO 6

pumpkin *loaf cake*

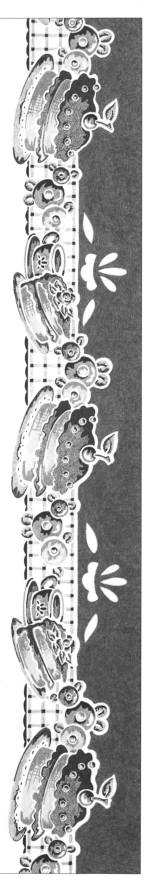

PUMPKIN CAKE MAKES FOR AN EASY AND scrumptious fall dessert. To dress it up, serve with cinnamon-scented whipped cream on the side.

1 1/4 cups all-purpose flour

1 teaspoon baking powder

1/2 teaspoon baking soda

1/2 teaspoon ground cinnamon

1/4 teaspoon ground allspice

1/4 teaspoon ground ginger

1/8 teaspoon freshly grated nutmeg

1/2 teaspoon salt

1/4 cup (1/2 stick) unsalted butter,
 at room temperature

1/2 cup packed dark brown sugar

1/2 cup granulated sugar

1/4 cup vegetable oil

2 large eggs, at room temperature

1 teaspoon vanilla extract

1 cup canned solid-pack pumpkin

1. Preheat the oven to 350°F. Grease and flour an 8 1/2-x 4 1/2-inch loaf pan.

2. In a medium bowl, whisk together the flour, baking powder, baking soda, cinnamon, allspice, ginger, nutmeg, and salt.

3. In a large bowl, beat the butter and both sugars with an electric mixer until light and fluffy. Beat in the oil. Add the eggs one at a time, beating well after each addition. Beat in the vanilla. On low speed, beat in the flour mixture, alternating with the pumpkin. Pour the batter into the prepared pan and smooth the top.

4. Bake the cake for 50 to 55 minutes, until a toothpick inserted into the center comes out clean. Let cool in the pan on a wire rack for 15 minutes. Remove the cake from the pan, set right side up on the rack, and let cool completely.

SERVES 8 TO 10

classic angel
food cake

I F YOU'VE NEVER TASTED HOMEMADE ANGEL food cake, you're in for a real treat! It is wonderfully light, tender and airy, something that's so often missing from store-bought cakes. Cooling this cake is quite a sight: you turn the pan upside down, and put the tube over a long-necked bottle, and suspend the cake on it. This helps the cake cool properly and keeps its edges from cooking further and becoming rubbery.

I cup sifted cake flour (not self-rising)

I 1/2 cups sugar

1/4 teaspoon salt

I 2 large egg whites, at room temperature

I 1/2 teaspoons cream of tartar

I 1/2 teaspoons vanilla extract

1. Preheat the oven to 325°F.

2. Sift together the flour, 3/4 cup of the sugar, and the salt.

3. In a very large bowl, beat the egg whites with an electric mixer until foamy. Add the cream of tartar and beat until soft peaks form. Beat in the remaining 3/4 cup sugar, about 2 tablespoons at a time and continue to beat until stiff, shiny peaks form.

4. Sift the flour mixture about 3 tablespoons at a time over the beaten whites and gently fold in the flour with a large rubber spatula just until incorporated. Fold in the vanilla.

5. Spoon the batter into an ungreased 10- x 4-inch tube pan, preferably with a removable bottom. Smooth the top with the rubber spatula, then run a long knife once through the batter to remove any large air pockets.

6. Bake the cake for 45 to 50 minutes, until light golden brown on top and a cake tester inserted into the center comes out clean. Invert the cake pan onto a long-necked bottle and let it cool completely.

7. Run a thin metal spatula around the edge of the cake and around the edge of the center tube to release the cake from the pan. Invert the cake onto a plate and remove the pan. Use a serrated knife to slice the cake.

SERVES 10 TO 12

very gingery. gingerbread

TINY PIECES OF CRYSTALLIZED GINGER GIVE this moist gingerbread a delightful bite. If you like frosting on your gingerbread, the Easy Buttercream Frosting on page 80 will add the perfect amount of sweetness to balance the spices.

2 1/2 cups all-purpose flour

2 teaspoons ground ginger

1/2 teaspoon ground allspice

1/2 teaspoon ground cinnamon

1/2 teaspoon freshly grated nutmeg

1/2 teaspoon baking soda

1/2 teaspoon salt

1 cup granulated sugar

1 cup molasses

3/4 cup (1 1/2 sticks) unsalted butter, melted and cooled

1/2 cup buttermilk or plain yogurt

1/2 cup milk

1 large egg, lightly beaten

1/4 cup minced crystallized ginger

Confectioners' sugar, for dusting

1. Preheat the oven to 350°F. Generously grease a 9-inch round or square baking pan.

2. In a large bowl, combine the flour, ground ginger, allspice, cinnamon, nutmeg, baking soda, and salt. Set aside.

3. In a medium bowl, whisk together the granulated sugar, molasses, melted butter, buttermilk, milk, and egg until smooth. With a wooden spoon, stir the molasses mixture into the flour mixture until the batter is smooth and thoroughly mixed. Stir in the crystallized ginger. Pour the batter into the prepared pan.

4. Bake the gingerbread for 40 minutes, or until a toothpick inserted into the center comes out clean. Let cool in the pan on a wire rack. Remove the cake from the pan and dust the top with confectioners' sugar.

SERVES 8

fancy white *layer cake*

a THREE-LAYER-TALL WHITE CAKE IS PERFECT for almost any special occasion. This one serves a lot of people, so bring it out for a party! For an extra touch, garnish each serving with fresh raspberries or strawberries or drizzle a little Raspberry Sauce (page 124) around each slice. If you prefer, you can substitute Seven-Minute Icing (page 70) for the buttercream frosting, but if so, serve the cake within several hours of frosting it. Using a standing electric mixer makes smooth work of this recipe.

WHITE CAKE

2 1/2 cups cake flour (not self-rising)

1 tablespoon baking powder

1/2 teaspoon salt

3/4 cup (1 1/2 sticks) unsalted butter,
   at room temperature

1 3/4 cups granulated sugar

1 1/2 teaspoons vanilla extract

1 cup milk

6 large egg whites, at room temperature

RICH BUTTERCREAM FROSTING

14 tablespoons (1 3/4 sticks) unsalted butter,
   at room temperature

4 1/2 cups confectioners' sugar

About 1/2 cup heavy cream

1 1/2 teaspoons vanilla extract

1. Make the white cake. Preheat the oven to 350°F. Grease and flour three 9-inch round cake pans.

2. Sift together the flour, baking powder, and salt into a large bowl and set aside.

3. In another large bowl, beat the butter and granulated sugar with an electric mixer until light and fluffy. Beat in the vanilla. On low speed, beat in the flour mixture in 3 additions, alternating with the milk in 2 additions.

4. In another large bowl, using clean beaters, beat the egg whites on low speed just until frothy. Increase the speed to high and beat just until stiff peaks form.

5. Using a large rubber spatula, fold about one quarter of the whites into the batter. Fold in the remaining whites in 2 or 3 additions, until just combined. Pour the batter into the prepared pans and smooth the tops.

6. Bake the layers for 23 to 25 minutes, until a toothpick inserted into the center comes out clean. Let cool in the pans on wire racks for 10 minutes. Remove the layers from the pans, set right side up on the racks, and let cool completely.

7. Make the rich buttercream frosting. In a large bowl, beat the butter with an electric mixer until light and fluffy. On low speed, beat in the confectioners' sugar, 7 tablespoons of the cream, and the vanilla. Increase the speed to high and beat until light and fluffy. If necessary, add another 1 to 2 tablespoons cream.

8. Place one of the cake layers on a serving plate. Reserve 1 cup of the frosting for decorating the top of the cake. Spread a thin layer of the remaining frosting over the top of the cake layer. Place the second layer on the top and spread with a thin layer of frosting. Place the third layer on top and frost the top and side of the cake.

9. Transfer the reserved frosting to a pastry bag fitted with a medium star tip and pipe several large rosettes on the top of the cake.

SERVES 12 TO 14

best all-american
chocolate cake

GLASS OF COLD MILK IS ALWAYS AN APPROPRIATE accompaniment to chocolate layer cake. But a scoop of vanilla ice cream (homemade Vanilla Bean Ice Cream, page 106, if you want to go all out) would of course be delicious too.

1 2/3 cups all-purpose flour

2/3 cup unsweetened cocoa powder,
   preferably Dutch-process

1 1/2 teaspoons baking powder

1/2 teaspoon baking soda

1/4 teaspoon salt

3/4 cup (1 1/2 sticks) unsalted butter,
   at room temperature

1 1/2 cups sugar

3 large eggs, at room temperature

1 1/2 teaspoons vanilla extract

1 1/3 cups sour cream

Chocolate Frosting or
   Sour Cream Fudge Frosting (p. 67)

1. Preheat the oven to 350°F. Grease and flour two 9-inch round cake pans.

2. In a large bowl, whisk together the flour, cocoa, baking powder, baking soda, and salt.

3. In a large bowl, beat the butter and sugar with an electric mixer until light and fluffy. Add in the eggs one at a time, beating well after each addition. Beat in the vanilla. On low speed, beat in half the flour mixture. Beat in the sour cream, then beat in the remaining flour mixture. Pour the batter into the prepared pans and smooth the tops.

4. Bake the layers for 28 to 30 minutes, until a toothpick inserted in the center comes out clean. Let cool in the pans on wire racks for 10 minutes. Remove the layers from the pans, set them right side up on the racks, and let cool completely.

5. Place one of the cake layers on a serving plate. Spread a generous layer of the frosting over the top. Place the second layer on top and frost the top and side of the cake with the remaining frosting. The cake can be made several hours ahead and set aside at cool room temperature.

SERVES 8 TO 10

german chocolate *cake*

HAPPY IS THE BIRTHDAY BOY OR GIRL WHO'S served this sweet, dark chocolate cake, topped with a creamy pecan-and-coconut frosting.

SWEET CHOCOLATE CAKE

2 1/4 cups all-purpose flour

1 teaspoon baking soda

1/4 teaspoon salt

1 cup (2 sticks) unsalted butter

1 1/2 cups granulated sugar

4 large eggs, separated

4 ounces sweet or semisweet chocolate, melted

2 teaspoons vanilla extract

1 cup buttermilk

COCONUT-PECAN ICING

1 cup evaporated milk

1/2 cup (1 stick) unsalted butter

1/2 cup packed dark brown sugar

2 large egg yolks

Pinch of salt

1 teaspoon vanilla extract

1 1/4 cups sweetened shredded coconut

1 cup chopped pecans

1. Make the sweet chocolate cake. Preheat the oven to 350°F. Grease and flour two 9-inch round cake pans.

2. Sift together the flour, baking soda, and salt and set aside.

3. In a large bowl, beat the butter and granulated sugar with an electric mixer until light and fluffy. Add the egg yolks, one at a time, beating well after each addition. Beat in the chocolate and vanilla. On low speed, beat in the flour mixture in two additions, alternating with the buttermilk.

4. In another large bowl, using clean beaters, beat the egg whites until stiff peaks form. Using a rubber spatula, gently fold the egg whites into the cake batter. Pour the batter into the prepared pans and gently smooth the tops.

5. Bake the cakes for 25 to 30 minutes, until a toothpick inserted into the center comes out clean. Let the cakes cool in the pans on wire racks for 10 minutes. Remove the cakes from the pans, set right side up on the racks, and let cool completely.

6. Meanwhile, make the coconut-pecan icing. In a medium saucepan, combine the milk, butter, and brown sugar over medium-low heat. Cook, stirring occasionally, until the sugar dissolves, about 5 minutes.

7. In a small bowl, beat the egg yolks and salt until smooth. Add a little of the milk mixture to the egg yolks, stirring constantly. Add the yolks to the milk mixture and cook, stirring constantly, for about 10 minutes, until the mixture lightly coats the back of the spoon. Stir in the vanilla and strain the mixture through a sieve into a clean bowl. Let cool.

8. Stir the coconut and pecans into the icing. Place one cake layer on a serving platter and spread frosting over the top. Place the second layer on top and frost with the remaining icing.

SERVES 12

devil's food *cupcakes*

C HILDREN WILL LOVE DECORATING THESE yummy and easy-to-make cupcakes. Tint the icing different colors and have a variety of colored sugar crystals, sprinkles, and mini chocolate candies on hand.

I 3/4 cups all-purpose flour

2/3 cup unsweetened cocoa powder

I 1/2 teaspoons baking soda

1/4 teaspoon salt

1/2 cup (I stick) unsalted butter,
    at room temperature

I 1/2 cups sugar

2 large eggs, at room temperature

I 1/2 teaspoons vanilla extract

I 1/3 cups buttermilk

Easy Buttercream Frosting (p. 70)

Food coloring (optional)

Sprinkles, mini M&M's, colored sugar, etc.,
    for decorating

1. Preheat the oven to 350°F. Line 20 muffin cups with foil liners.

2. In a medium bowl, whisk together the flour, cocoa, baking soda, and salt.

3. In a large bowl, beat the butter and sugar with an electric mixer until light and fluffy. Add the eggs one at a time, beating well after each addition. Beat in the vanilla. On low speed, add the flour mixture alternating with the buttermilk, beginning and ending with the flour mixture. Spoon the batter into the prepared muffin cups, filling each one about two-thirds full.

4. Bake the cupcakes for 17 to 19 minutes, until a toothpick inserted into the center of a cupcake comes out clean. Let cool completely in the pans on wire racks.

5. If desired, divide the frosting among several bowls and tint it different colors with food coloring: leave one bowl of frosting white. Ice the cupcakes generously with the frosting. Before the frosting has set, sprinkle the decorations on top.

MAKES 20 CUPCAKES

marble cake with *chocolate frosting*

F UN TO MAKE, THIS IS A DELECTABLE VERSION of a perennial favorite. Marbleizing is a simple technique that kids love. Simply spoon the batter into the pan and give them a popsicle stick to swirl it around!

2 cups plus 2 tablespoons all-purpose flour

1 1/2 teaspoons baking powder

1/2 teaspoon baking soda

1/2 teaspoon salt

10 tablespoons (1 1/4 sticks) unsalted butter,
   at room temperature

1 1/3 cups sugar

3 large eggs, at room temperature

1 1/2 teaspoons vanilla extract

1 cup milk

2 ounces semisweet chocolate, melted and cooled

Chocolate Frosting (p. 67) or

   Sour Cream Fudge Frosting (p. 67)

1. Preheat the oven to 350°F. Grease and flour two 9-inch round cake pans.

2. In a medium bowl, whisk together the flour, baking powder, baking soda, and salt.

3. In a large bowl, beat the butter and sugar with an electric mixer until light and fluffy. Add the eggs one at a time, beating well after each addition. Beat in the vanilla. On low speed, add in the flour mixture alternately with the milk.

4. Pour half the batter into another large bowl. With a rubber spatula, fold in the cooled chocolate. Spoon alternating dollops of the plain and chocolate batters into each prepared pan. With a knife, gently swirl the batter to marbleize it.

5. Bake the layers for 25 to 28 minutes, until a toothpick inserted into the center comes out clean. Let cool in the pans on wire racks for 10 minutes. Remove the layers from the pans, set right side up on the racks, and let cool completely.

6. Place one of the layers on a serving plate. Spread a generous layer of the frosting over the top. Place the second layer on top and frost the top and side of the cake with the remaining frosting. The cake can be made several hours ahead and set aside at cool room temperature.

SERVES 8 TO 10

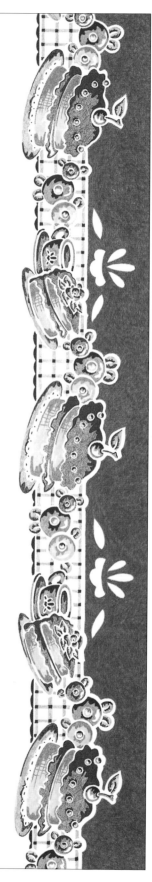

new york *cheesecake*

EW DESSERTS BEAT THE MELT-IN-YOUR MOUTH decadence of a good cheesecake. Fresh lemon zest is essential for adding the bite usually associated with cheesecake.

I 1/4 cups graham cracker crumbs

3 tablespoons brown sugar

5 tablespoons unsalted butter, melted and cooled

3 (8-ounce) packages cream cheese, at room temperature

I cup granulated sugar

I (8-ounce) container sour cream

3 large eggs

2 large egg yolks

I teaspoon vanilla extract

1/2 teaspoon grated lemon zest

1. Preheat the oven to 300°F. Generously grease a 9-inch round springform pan.

2. In a small bowl, stir together the graham cracker crumbs, brown sugar, and melted butter. Press the crumb mixture evenly over the bottom and up the side of the prepared pan and place in the refrigerator.

3. In a medium bowl, beat the cream cheese and granulated sugar with an electric mixer, for about 2 minutes, until light and fluffy. Beat in the sour cream until smooth. Add the eggs and egg yolks, one at a time, beating well after each addition.

Beat in the vanilla and lemon zest. Pour the batter into the prepared springform pan and smooth the top.

4. Bake the cake for 80 minutes, or until the center is set. Let the cake cool completely in the pan on a wire rack. Refrigerate for at least 2 hours before serving.

SERVES 10 TO 12

mocha *cheesecake*

HIS RICH, DARK CHEESECAKE REALLY NEEDS no adornment, but you could garnish it with grated or shaved chocolate to hint at its seductive flavor. Baking the cake in a "water bath" keeps it wonderfully creamy.

CHOCOLATE COOKIE CRUST

1 1/3 cups chocolate cookie crumbs

5 tablespoons unsalted butter, melted

MOCHA FILLING

1 tablespoon instant coffee granules

2 teaspoons vanilla extract

3 (8-ounce) packages cream cheese,
    at room temperature

1 cup sugar

3 large eggs, at room temperature

1 (8-ounce) container sour cream

6 ounces semisweet chocolate, melted and cooled

1. Preheat the oven to 325°F. Wrap the outside of a 9-inch round springform pan with a double layer of heavy-duty foil, making sure there are no holes or tears in the foil.

2. Make the chocolate cookie crust. In a small bowl, stir together the cookie crumbs and melted butter. Press the crumb mixture evenly over the bottom of the prepared pan and place in the refrigerator.

3. Make the mocha filling. In a small cup, combine the coffee and vanilla and stir to dissolve the coffee.

4. In a large bowl, preferably the bowl of a standing mixer, beat the cream cheese until fluffy. Beat in the sugar. Add the eggs one at a time, beating well after each addition. Beat in the sour cream, then the cooled chocolate and the coffee mixture. Pour the batter into the prepared springform pan and smooth the top.

5. Set the pan in a large roasting pan and add enough very hot water to the roasting pan to come one-third up the side of the springform.

6. Bake the cheesecake for 75 minutes, or until the top is slightly puffed and the center is just firm to the touch. Turn off the oven, prop the oven door ajar with a wooden spoon, and let the cake cool in the oven for 1 hour.

7. Remove the cheesecake from the water and remove the foil. Set the pan on a wire rack to cool completely, then cover and refrigerate for at least 6 hours, or overnight.

8. To serve, run a thin knife around the edge of the cake and remove the pan sides. Cut the cake into wedges, wiping the knife clean between cuts.

SERVES 10 TO 12

flourless chocolate *soufflé cake*

t HIS DARK CHOCOLATE, SOFT-CENTERED SOUFFLE cake is a light-textured alternative to dense flourless chocolate tortes. Serve it alone, or with a scoop of vanilla ice cream.

1/2 cup (1 stick) unsalted butter

8 ounces bittersweet chocolate, coarsely chopped

4 large eggs, at room temperature

1 large egg yolk, at room temperature

1/2 cup granulated sugar

1 teaspoon vanilla extract

1/4 teaspoon salt

2 teaspoons cornstarch

Confectioners' sugar, for dusting

1. Preheat the oven to 375°F. Generously grease and sugar (or dust with cocoa powder) a 9-inch round springform pan.

2. In a small saucepan, combine the butter and chocolate and melt over low heat, stirring until smooth. Transfer to a large bowl and let cool to room temperature.

3. In a medium bowl, beat the eggs, egg yolk, granulated sugar, vanilla, and salt with an electric mixer at high speed until tripled in volume and light in color, about 5 minutes. Scrape the mixture into the melted chocolate and butter and sift the cornstarch on top. Gently fold the egg mixture into the chocolate mixture until combined. Pour the batter into the prepared pan.

4. Bake the cake for 25 to 30 minutes, until it has puffed, has a thin crust on top, and jiggles slightly at the center when shaken very gently. Let the cake rest for 5 minutes before removing the sides of the pan. Dust with confectioners' sugar and serve immediately.

SERVES 8

89

carrot cake with *cream cheese frosting*

C ARROTS LEND THIS CAKE LOTS OF MOISTURE. That, and the subtle blend of sweetness and spice, makes this a perennial favorite.

CARROT CAKE

1 3/4 cups all-purpose flour

2 teaspoons baking powder

1 teaspoon baking soda

1 teaspoon ground cinnamon

1/2 teaspoon ground ginger

1/2 teaspoon ground allspice

1 teaspoon salt

4 large eggs, at room temperature

1 cup granulated sugar

1 cup packed light brown sugar

1 cup plus 2 tablespoons vegetable oil

2 teaspoons vanilla extract

4 cups grated or shredded carrots (about 1 pound)

1 cup walnuts, coarsely chopped

CREAM CHEESE FROSTING

1 (8-ounce) package cream cheese, at room temperature

1/4 cup (1/2 stick) unsalted butter, at room temperature

1 1/2 teaspoons vanilla extract

2 1/2 cups confectioners' sugar

1. Make the carrot cake. Preheat the oven to 350°F. Grease two 9-inch round cake pans. Line the bottoms with waxed paper; grease and flour the paper.

2. In a medium bowl, whisk together the flour, baking powder, baking soda, cinnamon, ginger, allspice and salt. Set aside.

3. In a large bowl, beat the eggs with an electric mixer until frothy. Gradually beat in the granulated and brown sugars. Beat in the oil and vanilla until thoroughly blended.

4. On low speed, beat in the flour mixture in two additions. With a large wooden spoon, stir in the carrots and walnuts. Pour the batter into the prepared pans, distributing the carrots and nuts evenly.

5. Bake the layers for 75 minutes, or until a toothpick inserted into the center comes out clean. Let cool in the pans on wire racks for 15 minutes. Remove the layers from the pans, invert the layers and remove the waxed paper, then set them right side up on the racks and let cool completely.

6. Make the cream cheese frosting. In a medium bowl, beat the cream cheese and butter with an electric mixer until light and fluffy. Beat in the vanilla. Gradually beat in the confectioners' sugar until smooth and shiny.

7. Place one layer on a serving plate and spread a thin layer of frosting over the top. Place the second layer on top and frost the top and side of the cake. Refrigerate until serving.

SERVES 10 TO 12

Chapter Five

comfort in a spoon

rice pudding *with raisins*

tHIS CREAMY STOVE-TOP RICE PUDDING IS perfect comfort food. Each mouthful is gently spiced with cinnamon, mace, and lemon and studded with sweet golden raisins.

3 1/4 cups milk

1 cup heavy cream

2/3 cup sugar

2 strips lemon zest (removed with a
   vegetable peeler)

1/2 teaspoon ground cinnamon

1/4 teaspoon ground mace

1/8 teaspoon salt

2/3 cup long-grain white rice

1/2 cup golden raisins

2 large egg yolks

2 teaspoons vanilla extract

1. In a large heavy saucepan, combine 3 cups milk, the cream, sugar, lemon zest, cinnamon, mace, and salt. Bring the mixture to a simmer over medium high heat. Stir in the rice, cover the pan, and simmer gently over very low heat for 45 minutes, stirring occasionally.

2. Add the raisins and continue to simmer gently, stirring occasionally, for about 30 minutes, until the rice is tender and almost all of the milk has been absorbed. Remove the lemon zest.

3. In a small bowl, whisk together the egg yolks and the remaining 1/4 cup milk. Stir into the pudding and cook very gently for 2 to 3 minutes, stirring constantly, until it thickens slightly. Remove the pan from the heat and stir in the vanilla. Let the pudding cool slightly.

4. Transfer the pudding to a serving bowl and cover with a piece of plastic wrap directly touching the surface of the pudding. Refrigerate for at least 2 hours before serving.

SERVES 6

butterscotch *pudding*

tHIS CREAMY GOLDEN CLASSIC PUDDING IS the very definition of indulgence. The dark brown sugar gives it the old-fashioned taste that takes you back to your grandma's kitchen.

> 3 cups milk
>
> 4 large egg yolks
>
> 3/4 cup packed dark brown sugar
>
> 1/4 cup cornstarch
>
> 2 tablespoons cold unsalted butter, cut in pieces
>
> 2 teaspoons vanilla extract

1. In a heavy medium saucepan, bring 2 1/2 cups milk to a simmer over medium heat.

2. Meanwhile, whisk together the remaining 1/2 cup milk, the egg yolks, brown sugar, and cornstarch until smooth.

3. Gradually whisk about 1 cup of the hot milk into the egg yolk mixture until well incorporated. Pour the egg yolk mixture into the saucepan of hot milk and bring to a simmer, whisking constantly. Simmer, whisking, for 2 minutes. Remove the pan from the heat and whisk in the butter and vanilla.

4. Pass the pudding through a strainer set over a serving bowl. Let cool completely, then cover with plastic wrap directly touching the surface and refrigerate for at least 2 to 3 hours before serving.

SERVES 6

tapioca *pudding*

yOU'LL ADORE THIS PUDDING, WHICH IS THE creamiest and richest of its kind.

> 3 cups milk
>
> 2/3 cup quick-cooking tapioca
>
> Pinch of salt
>
> 3 large egg yolks
>
> 1/2 cup sugar
>
> 1 1/2 teaspoons vanilla extract

1. In a heavy medium saucepan, bring the milk, tapioca, and salt to a simmer over medium-high heat. Lower the heat to medium-low and simmer the mixture for 3 to 4 minutes, until the tapioca is soft.

2. Meanwhile, in a bowl, stir together the egg yolks and sugar until smooth.

3. Gradually whisk about 1 cup of the hot tapioca into the egg yolk mixture until well incorporated. Pour the egg yolk mixture into the saucepan of hot tapioca and bring to a simmer, stirring constantly. Simmer, stirring, for 2 minutes. Remove the saucepan from the heat and stir in the vanilla.

4. Transfer the pudding to a serving bowl. Let cool completely, then cover with plastic wrap directly touching the surface and refrigerate for at least 2 to 3 hours before serving.

SERVES 6

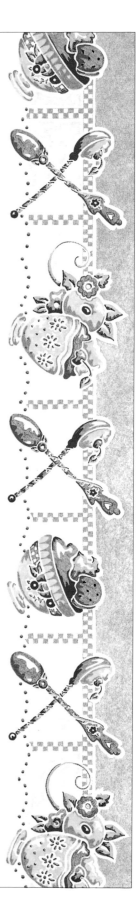

rich chocolate *pudding*

tHE DOUBLE HIT OF COCOA AND CHOCOLATE gives this pudding its particularly intense flavor.

2 1/4 cups milk

1/2 cup sugar

Pinch of salt

3 tablespoons unsweetened cocoa powder

2 tablespoons cornstarch

2 large egg yolks

1 large egg

1 (6-ounce) package semisweet chocolate chips, melted and cooled

1 tablespoon vanilla extract

1. In a medium saucepan, combine the milk, sugar, and salt over medium-high heat. Bring the mixture to a boil, stirring constantly. Sift the cocoa and cornstarch into the hot milk mixture. Using a whisk, beat the mixture until it is very smooth. Cook, whisking constantly, until it reaches a boil, then continue whisking for 1 minute. Remove the saucepan from the heat and set aside.

2. In a small bowl, whisk together the egg yolks and egg until frothy. Gradually whisk a few tablespoons of the hot pudding mixture into the beaten eggs until well combined. Pour the egg mixture in to the saucepan of hot pudding mixture. Whisk until well blended and smooth.

3. Return the saucepan to low heat and cook the pudding, whisking constantly, for about 2 minutes, until it thickens slightly. Remove the pan from the heat and stir in the cooled chocolate and the vanilla.

4. Divide the pudding mixture among 4 small serving bowls or parfait glasses. Cover them with plastic wrap directly touching the surface and refrigerate until cold, about 3 hours, or up to 4 days.

SERVES 4

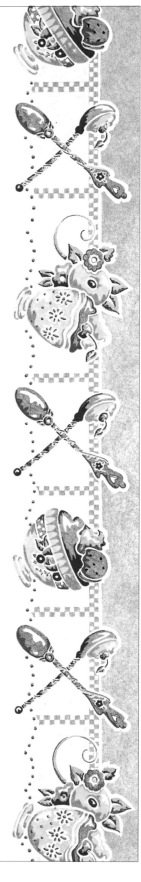

bittersweet chocolate
bread pudding

ARK BITTERSWEET CHOCOLATE ADDS A TOUCH of glamour to this comforting bread pudding. Good chocolate is what makes this pudding stand out from the rest, so buy the highest-quality you can find, such as Valrhona, Callebaut, or Ghirardelli.

2 cups heavy cream

8 ounces bittersweet chocolate,
   finely chopped

16 slices homemade-style white bread,
   crusts removed

1 cup milk

1/2 cup sugar

5 large eggs

1 teaspoon vanilla extract

Pinch of salt

1. In a medium saucepan, bring the cream to a simmer. Add the chocolate and turn off the heat. Let the mixture stand for 2 minutes, then whisk until the chocolate is melted.

2. Cut the bread slices in half and place in an 8-inch square baking pan.

3. In a medium bowl, whisk together the milk, sugar, eggs, vanilla, and salt. Add the chocolate mixture and whisk until smooth. Pour the mixture evenly over the bread. Cover with plastic wrap and refrigerate for 2 hours.

4. Preheat the oven to 350°F. Remove the pudding from the refrigerator, take off the plastic wrap, and press the bread down hard with a rubber spatula. Bake the pudding for 35 to 40 minutes, until the top is puffed and center is set. Transfer the pan to a wire rack to let cool slightly before serving. Serve warm, at room temperature, or cold.

SERVES 8

crème *brûlée*

THESE RICH SILKY-SMOOTH CUSTARDS TOPPED with a thin, crisp layer of caramel are the height of luxury—just the thing to complete a formal party. Crème brûlée dishes are available at speciality cookware shops, but you can also prepare the recipe using 6-ounce ramekins. Increase the baking time to about 50 minutes, and reduce the sugar for sprinkling to 3 tablespoons. The easiest way to caramelize the sugar topping is to use a household blowtorch, but the broiler also does a good job.

> **6 large egg yolks**
>
> **1/2 cup sugar, plus 5 tablespoons for sprinkling**
>
> **3 cups heavy cream**
>
> **1 teaspoon vanilla extract**

1. Position a rack in the center of the oven; preheat the oven to 300°F. Place 8 oval crème brûlée dishes in a large baking pan (use 2 pans if necessary).

2. In a large bowl, whisk the egg yolks and 1/2 cup sugar until thick and pale.

3. Meanwhile, in a large saucepan, bring the cream to the boil.

4. Whisking constantly, gradually add the hot cream to the egg yolk mixture and whisk until thoroughly blended. Strain the custard through a fine strainer into a large bowl. Stir in the vanilla.

5. Ladle or pour the custard into the dishes, filling them almost to the top. Carefully pour enough very hot water into the baking pan to come halfway up the sides of the dishes (you may find it easier to set the baking pan on the oven rack and then add the water).

6. Bake the custards for 40 minutes, or until just set; the centers should wiggle very slightly if shaken.

7. Let the custards cool in the water bath for 10 minutes, then using a wide spatula and an oven mitt, transfer the dishes to a wire rack to cool to room temperature. Refrigerate for at least 3 hours, until chilled, or overnight.

8. Preheat the broiler. Sprinkle the remaining 5 tablespoons sugar evenly over the tops of the custards. Arrange the dishes on a baking sheet, place under the broiler as close to the heat as possible, and broil for about 1 minute, until the sugar is caramelized. Using tongs or an oven mitt, carefully move or rotate the dishes as necessary so the sugar caramelizes evenly.

9. Let the custards sit for 1 to 2 minutes before serving. (The custards can be refrigerated for up to 1 hour, but no more, or the caramel may melt, before serving.)

SERVES 8

english *trifle*

HIS IS A GREAT DISH TO SERVE AT A PARTY but it does have to be started up to a day ahead. In England it is a staple at the Christmas table. Each family seems to have its own recipe handed down from generation to generation, but creamy custard layered with fruit and surrounded by cake and whipped cream are the constants. For this recipe, you can use store-bought pound cake, but, if you have the time, a homebaked one, like Rich Vanilla Pound Cake (page 71) would be ideal.

CUSTARD FILLING

2 cups half-and-half

1/3 cup granulated sugar

2 tablespoons cornstarch

4 large egg yolks

Pinch of salt

1 teaspoon vanilla extract

2 cups strawberries, sliced, or raspberries

1 (14-ounce) pound cake, cut in 1 1/2-inch cubes

1/2 cup cream sherry or orange juice

1 cup heavy cream

2 tablespoons confectioners' sugar

Mint leaves or candied violets, for garnish

1. Make the custard filling. In a medium saucepan, bring the half-and-half to a boil over medium-high heat. Remove the saucepan from the heat.

2. In a small bowl, stir together the granulated sugar, cornstarch, egg yolks, and salt. Gradually whisk 2 tablespoons of the hot half-and-half into the egg yolk mixture until well incorporated. Pour the egg yolk mixture into the saucepan of hot half-and-half, whisking well. Return the saucepan to low heat and cook the custard, stirring constantly, for 5 to 7 minutes, until it is thick. Do not let the mixture come to a boil.

3. Pour the custard through a strainer set over a large bowl, pressing on the solids with the back of a wooden spoon to extract as much of the liquid as possible; discard the solids. Whisk in the vanilla and let the custard cool completely. Cover with plastic wrap directly touching the surface and refrigerate for at least 2 hours.

4. Reserve a few of the strawberries for garnish. Place the cake cubes in a large bowl and add the cream sherry, tossing well to coat the cake. Place half the cake cubes in the bottom of a glass serving bowl. Top with half the strawberries and half the chilled custard. Repeat layering with remaining cake cubes, strawberries, and custard.

5. In a medium bowl, whip the cream and the confectioners' sugar with an electric mixer until soft peaks form. Spoon the whipped cream on top of the trifle and smooth the top with a rubber spatula. Cover with plastic wrap and refrigerate for at least 4 hours and up to 24 hours. Garnish the trifle with the reserved strawberries and mint leaves just before serving.

SERVES 8 TO 10

banana *betty*

SLICED BANANAS SMOTHERED WITH A CREAMY custard are contrasted with crunchy, crumbled spicy-sweet cookies in this classic pudding.

24 gingersnap cookies (6 ounces)

5 tablespoons sugar

2 tablespoons unsalted butter, melted

4 bananas

2 cups half-and-half

3 large egg yolks

1 teaspoon vanilla extract

1/2 teaspoon ground cinnamon

1. Preheat the oven to 350°F.

2. In a food processor, pulse the gingersnaps until coarsely ground. Add 2 tablespoons of the sugar and the butter and pulse until just combined.

3. Sprinkle half the crumbs over the bottom of an ungreased 8-inch cake pan or 1-quart casserole.

4. Peel and slice the bananas into 1/4-inch-thick slices and layer them over the crumb mixture.

5. In a small bowl, whisk together the half-and-half, egg yolks, remaining 3 tablespoons sugar, vanilla, and cinnamon. Pour the custard over the bananas and sprinkle the remaining crumb mixture on top.

6. Set the cake pan in a roasting pan. Carefully pour enough very hot water water into the roasting pan to come halfway up the sides of the cake pan.

7. Bake the betty until the center is just set (it should wiggle slightly). Remove the betty from the water bath and let cool on a wire rack before serving. Serve warm or at room temperature.

SERVES 4 TO 6

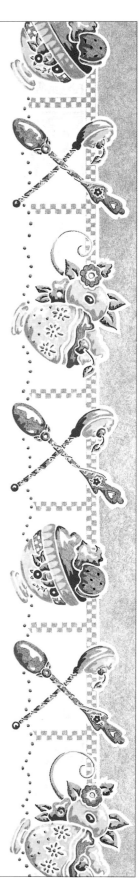

raspberry *fool*

SOME OF THE BEST DESSERTS ARE THE SIMPLEST and allow the flavors of the ingredients to really shine. Here sweet raspberries are combined with rich, luscious whipped cream. Whole raspberries garnish the top to hint at the flavor of the fool. Serve in wide-mouthed wineglasses or a clear glass serving bowl to show off the colorful cream.

> **1 cup raspberries**
>
> **3 tablespoons sugar, or more to taste**
>
> **1 cup heavy cream**

1. Reserve a few of the whole raspberries for garnish. In a food processor, combine about 3/4 cup of the raspberries and 2 tablespoons of the sugar and process to a smooth puree. Add more sugar to taste, if desired.

2. In a large bowl, beat the cream with the remaining 1 tablespoon sugar just until stiff peaks form. Gently fold the raspberry puree and half of the remaining whole raspberries into the whipped cream. Do not overfold; there should still be some streaks of white cream. Transfer to wineglasses or a serving bowl and refrigerate for 30 minutes, or until ready to serve.

3. Just before serving, scatter the reserved whole raspberries over the top of the fool.

SERVES 4

almost-instant *chocolate mousse*

m ADE IN MINUTES, WITH ONLY THREE INGREDIENTS, this easy mousse will satisfy even the most demanding chocolate lover. To dress it up, serve in individual glass dishes and garnish with dollops of sweetened whipped cream and whole raspberries.

8 ounces bittersweet or semisweet chocolate, coarsely chopped

1 1/2 cups heavy cream

1 teaspoon vanilla extract

1. In the top of a double boiler over barely simmering water, melt the chocolate, stirring occasionally until smooth. Remove from the heat and let cool slightly, just until tepid.

2. Meanwhile, in a large bowl, combine the cream and vanilla and beat with an electric mixer until soft peaks form. Using a large rubber spatula, fold in the chocolate.

3. Transfer to a serving bowl. Cover with plastic wrap and refrigerate for at least 30 minutes before serving.

SERVES 6

QUEEN OF THE KITCHEN TIP

Crème de la Crème

Simple creamy desserts like mousses, custards, and puddings make a perfect canvas for your favorite decorative or finishing touches. Whipped cream may be all that a rich pudding needs, but berries, as suggested here, can be delicious. A strip or two of candied citrus zest makes a sleek, elegant garnish. Chopped nuts of all kinds or even crushed Almond Brittle (page 143) would be a delicious topping, or try other crushed candies, perhaps peppermints or even lemon drops. Mint sprigs are an easy way to add a touch of color. Crystallized violets or rose petals (available in gourmet shops) are a classic garnish for chocolate mousse, or you could even dress up a creamy dessert with an edible (organic and not sprayed) flower blossom or two.

Chapter Six
cooling off

vanilla bean
ice cream

OMEMADE ICE CREAM IS SO SUPERIOR TO store-bought, once you indulge you may never go back! The consistency is creamier and more dense, and it has a flavor that will transport you back to your childhood. Vanilla beans impart a deeper, more intense flavor than the extract; you can find them at gourmet shops and many supermarkets.

COOLING OFF

2 cups heavy cream

1 cup milk

1 vanilla bean, sliced lengthwise

6 large egg yolks

3/4 cup plus 2 tablespoons sugar

1. Combine the cream and milk in a large heavy saucepan. Using the tip of a small sharp knife, scrape the seeds out of the vanilla bean into the saucepan. Add the pod and bring the cream mixture just to a simmer over medium heat.

2. Meanwhile, combine the egg yolks and sugar in a medium bowl and whisk until thick and smooth.

3. Whisking constantly, gradually add about half the hot cream mixture to the yolks, then pour the mixture into the saucepan of hot cream. Cook over medium-low heat, stirring constantly with a wooden spoon, until the custard thickens slightly and coats the back of the spoon (when you run your finger down the back of the spoon, it will leave a path; do not let boil).

4. Immediately remove the pan from the heat and strain the custard through a fine-mesh strainer into a medium bowl. Let cool, stirring occasionally. Cover and refrigerate for at least 2 hours, until chilled, or overnight.

5. Freeze the mixture in an ice cream maker according to the manufacturer's instructions. Transfer the ice cream to an airtight container and store in the freezer until ready to serve.

SERVES 6 TO 8

QUEEN OF THE KITCHEN TIP

Designer Ice Cream

Just like the ice cream parlor, you can customize your homemade ice cream with all sorts of mix-ins. Add chopped chocolate to vanilla or chocolate ice cream for chocolate chunk ice cream. Try crushed peppermints for mint chip. Cut up peanut butter cups or chocolate toffee bars are also delicious additions. In summer, add fresh raspberries or cut-up strawberries. The possibilities are almost limitless. For the recipes in this book, use about a cup or so of your chosen mix-in. Don't add it until the ice cream is ready, though, or the mix-in might freeze too hard (especially true of berries) or be overblended; add it to the machine at the last minute and let it churn for just a few seconds, until blended.

bittersweet chocolate
ice cream

HIS DEEP-DARK CHOCOLATE ICE CREAM IS delicious as is, but it's also good with the "mix-in" of your choice, such as chopped chocolate, crushed chocolate sandwich cookies, finely chopped dried cherries, or even minced candied ginger. Add them right before the ice cream is frozen and allow the machine to run a minute or so longer, just until well mixed. Use the sharp chef's knife and a firmly secured cutting board to chop chocolate.

8 ounces bittersweet chocolate, finely chopped

1 1/2 cups heavy cream

1 1/2 cups milk

6 large egg yolks

1 cup sugar

Pinch of salt

2 teaspoons vanilla extract

1. Place the chocolate in a large bowl. Combine the cream and milk in a large heavy saucepan and bring just to a simmer over medium heat.

2. Meanwhile, combine the egg yolks, sugar, and salt in a medium bowl and whisk until thick and smooth.

3. Whisking constantly, gradually add about half the cream mixture to the egg yolks, then pour the mixture into the saucepan of hot cream. Cook over medium-low heat, stirring constantly with a wooden spoon, until the custard thickens slightly and coats the back of the spoon (when you run your finger down the back of the spoon, it will leave a path; do not let boil).

4. Immediately remove the pan from the heat and pour the custard over the chocolate. Let sit for 30 seconds, then whisk until the chocolate is completely melted. Strain the custard through a fine-mesh strainer into a bowl. Stir in the vanilla. Let cool slightly, stirring occasionally, then cover and refrigerate for at least 2 hours, until chilled, or overnight.

5. Freeze the mixture in an ice cream maker according to the manufacturer's instructions. Transfer the ice cream to an airtight container and store in the freezer until ready to serve.

SERVES 6 TO 8

raspberry ice *cream*

COOLING OFF

F YOU LOVE THE COMBINATION OF TART, JUICY raspberries and luscious custard, you'll love this raspberry ice cream. Drizzling it with raspberry sauce (page 124) makes the flavors even more intense.

> **3 cups fresh, or thawed frozen, raspberries**
> **1 1/4 cups heavy cream**
> **4 large egg yolks**
> **1 cup sugar**
> **Pinch of salt**

1. In a food processor or blender, process the raspberries until pureed. Press them through a fine strainer set over a medium bowl to remove the seeds. Discard the seeds and reserve the puree.

2. Place a strainer over a medium bowl. Set aside.

3. In a large, heavy saucepan, bring the cream to a simmer. Remove from the heat.

4. In a medium bowl, using a wooden spoon, stir together the egg yolks, sugar, and salt until very smooth. Pour one-fourth of the hot cream into the yolk mixture, stirring constantly and vigorously. Stir in one-fourth more of the hot cream, then pour the egg-cream mixture into the saucepan.

5. Set the saucepan over medium-low heat and gently cook the custard, stirring constantly, until it thickens slightly and coats the back of the spoon (when you run your finger down the back of the spoon, it will leave a path; do not let boil).

6. When the custard has thickened, immediately remove the pan from the heat and pour the custard through the strainer into the bowl. Whisk the reserved raspberry puree into the custard.

7. Cover the bowl and refrigerate the custard for at least 4 hours, until chilled, or up to 2 days.

8. Freeze the mixture in an ice cream maker according to the manufacturer's instructions. Transfer the ice cream to an air-tight container and store in the freezer until ready to serve.

SERVES 6 TO 8

lemon. *ice*

dark chocolate *sorbet*

a COOL FLAVORED ICE IS WONDERFULLY refreshing on a hot summer evening. This recipe is very easy—you don't even need an ice cream maker. For grown-ups, drizzle a little limoncello (an Italian lemon-flavored liqueur) over each serving.

> 2 cups water
>
> 1 cup sugar
>
> 2 teaspoons grated lemon zest
>
> 2/3 cup fresh lemon juice (from about
>
>   3 lemons)
>
> Fresh mint sprigs, for garnish (optional)

1. Put a 9-inch square baking pan in the freezer to chill.

2. In a medium saucepan, combine the water, sugar, and lemon zest. Bring to a boil over medium heat, stirring to dissolve the sugar. Remove the saucepan from the heat and stir in the lemon juice. Let cool completely.

3. Pour the lemon mixture into the chilled baking pan and freeze for 4 to 6 hours, stirring once or twice with a fork, until frozen solid. (The lemon ice can be made up to a day ahead.)

4. To serve, break up the frozen ice into crystals with a fork. Spoon the ice into stemmed glasses, garnish each one with a mint sprig, if desired, and serve immediately.

SERVES 6 TO 8

b ECAUSE SORBETS DON'T CONTAIN EGGS OR cream, they are much lighter than ice cream. That doesn't mean to say they sacrifice any flavor. The combination of bittersweet chocolate and cocoa powder gives this sorbet a wonderfully intense, chocolatey taste.

> 4 ounces bittersweet chocolate, finely chopped
>
> 2 cups water
>
> 1 cup sugar
>
> 1/2 cup unsweetened cocoa powder
>
> 1/2 teaspoon vanilla extract

1. Place the chocolate in a medium bowl. In a medium heavy saucepan, combine the water and sugar and bring to a boil over medium heat, stirring to dissolve the sugar. Reduce the heat to low and add the cocoa, whisking until completely blended and smooth.

2. Pour the cocoa syrup over the chocolate and let stand for 30 seconds, then whisk gently until the chocolate is completely melted. Let cool slightly, stirring occasionally. Refrigerate for at least 2 hours, until chilled, or overnight.

3. Freeze the mixture in an ice cream maker according to the manufacturer's instructions. Transfer to an airtight container and store in the freezer for 2 to 3 hours, or overnight, before serving.

SERVES 6

almond peach *sherbet*

AKING SORBETS AND SHERBETS FROM FROZEN cans of fruit in syrup is about as easy as a recipe can be . . . with delicious results. Here, a touch of amaretto (almond flavored-liqueur) adds a more adult taste. If you prefer substitute a few drops of almond extract.

1 (15-ounce) can peaches in heavy syrup

1/4 cup milk

2 1/2 tablespoons superfine sugar

1 tablespoon amaretto

1. Place the can of peaches in the freezer for at least 4 hours, or until frozen solid.

2. In a small bowl, dissolve the sugar in the milk. Hold the frozen can of peaches under hot running water for about 20 seconds, then open the can and place its contents into the bowl of a food processor.

3. Add the milk mixture and amaretto to the bowl and process until smooth, about 1 minute. Serve immediately or transfer to an airtight container and freeze until ready to serve.

SERVES 3 TO 4

Ice Cream & Company

Ice cream is our favorite frozen dessert, but it's only one member of a popular family. Ice cream may be made with just milk and/or cream, sugar, and flavoring, or it may also include an egg-custard base, making it rich and creamier, in which case it is known as French-style ice cream. Sherbet, ice cream's closest cousin, is a frozen fruit ice, sweetened with sugar, that may contain some milk or gelatin; egg whites are often added for a smoother texture. Sorbet, one of our more recent passions, is a smooth ice most commonly made with fruit juice and a sugar syrup, never with milk or any other dairy products. Granitas and ices are similar to sorbets, but are generally more granular in texture; they are usually either stirred as they freeze or broken up (or shaved) once frozen to create larger ice crystals.

espresso *granita*

RANITAS, ICES SERVED IN CORNER CAFÉS and restaurants throughout Italy, are gaining popularity on this side of the Atlantic. The freezing-and-stirring process is the traditional method of preparation. However, you can also allow the mixture to freeze until solid, without stirring, then break it into chunks and process briefly in a food processor to the consistency of shaved ice, and serve immediately. If you like, garnish this sophisticated coffee granita with a twist of lemon peel or a dollop of whipped cream. You could also add a splash of Sambuca, or other anise-flavored liqueur, to each serving.

2/3 cup finely ground espresso beans

1/2 cup sugar

3 cups boiling water

1. Put a 13- x 9-inch baking pan in the freezer to chill.

2. Combine the ground espresso beans and sugar in a medium bowl. Add the boiling water and stir to dissolve the sugar. Let stand for 15 minutes.

3. Pour the mixture through a strainer lined with a coffee filter (or a double thickness of cheesecloth) into a medium bowl. Let cool.

4. Pour the mixture into the chilled baking pan and freeze for 30 minutes, or until ice crystals begin to form around the sides of the pan. Using a fork, stir the crystals into the mixture in the center of the pan, breaking up any large chunks. Freeze for about 2 1/2 hours longer, stirring every 30 minutes, until the granita is completely frozen. (The granita can be made early in the day and kept frozen until ready to serve.)

5. Scrape the granita into stemmed glasses or bowls and serve immediately.

SERVES 4 TO 6

chocolate strawberry
parfait pie

HIS SUBLIME DESSERT COMBINES A chocolate graham cracker and almond crust, layers of strawberry and vanilla ice cream, hot fudge sauce, whipped cream, and fresh strawberries. We swirl the hot fudge sauce into the top layer of ice cream to give the pie a very professional look.

CHOCOLATE–GRAHAM CRACKER CRUST

10 full sheets chocolate graham crackers

3/4 cup whole unblanched almonds

1/4 cup (1/2 stick) unsalted butter, melted

1 tablespoon packed brown sugar

1 teaspoon vanilla extract

CHOCOLATE–STRAWBERRY FILLING

1 pint strawberry ice cream, softened

1 pint vanilla ice cream, softened

1/2 cup Best-Ever Hot Fudge Sauce (p. 124)

Whipped cream, for garnish

Strawberries, hulled and sliced, for garnish

1. Preheat the oven to 375°F.

2. Make the chocolate–graham cracker crust. In a food processor, grind the graham crackers and almonds until the mixture resembles fine crumbs. Add the butter, sugar, and vanilla and pulse to combine. Using your fingers, lightly but firmly press enough of the crumb mixture evenly over the bottom and up the side of a 9-inch pie plate. Set the unused crumb mixture aside. Bake the crumb crust for 6 minutes. Let the crust cool on a wire rack completely.

3. Make the chocolate-strawberry filling. Spread the strawberry ice cream evenly over the crumb crust, smoothing with a metal spatula. Sprinkle the remaining crumb mixture evenly over the ice cream. Spread the vanilla ice cream over the crumb layer. Cover the pie with plastic wrap and freeze for 1 hour.

4. Pour the fudge sauce into a bowl and microwave on high power for about 15 seconds, until pourable. Cover the pie evenly with the fudge sauce. Using the handle of a wooden spoon, swirl the fudge sauce into the vanilla ice cream. Freeze the pie for 4 hours, or until firm.

5. Just before serving, garnish the pie with whipped cream and strawberries.

SERVES 8

frozen *mochaccino*

MILK SHAKES FOR GROWN-UPS? THESE frosty coolers feature coffee three ways—instant espresso powder, coffee ice cream, and coffee liqueur.

2 cups milk

1 tablespoon instant espresso powder

3 tablespoons coffee-flavored liqueur

1 pint coffee ice cream, slightly softened

1 pint chocolate ice cream, slightly softened

Whipped cream, for garnish

Cinnamon, for sprinkling

1. In a small bowl, combine 1/4 cup of the milk and the espresso powder and stir to dissolve the espresso.

2. In a blender, combine half the espresso mixture, half the remaining milk, 1 1/2 tablespoons liqueur, and half the coffee and chocolate ice creams. Blend on high speed until smooth. Transfer to a large pitcher. Repeat with the remaining espresso mixture, milk, liqueur, and ice creams.

3. Fill 6 tall glasses with ice and pour the ice cream mixture into them. Garnish each glass with a generous dollop of the whipped cream and sprinkle the cinnamon over the top. Serve immediately, with long-handled spoons.

S E R V E S   6

ice cream *sandwiches*

ICE CREAM SANDWICHES ARE A PERENNIAL favorite with all ages. We offer a basic recipe, use it as a basis for your own interpretations. Try chunky chocolate chip cookies instead of plain chocolate, use one or more different ice creams, roll the sides of the sandwiches in toasted coconut or chopped toasted almonds, or even crushed peppermint candies—whatever takes your fancy.

2 pints vanilla ice cream, slightly softened

16 large (about 3 1/2 inches in diameter) chocolate cookies

1 cup mini semisweet chocolate chips

1. Spread 1/2 cup of the ice cream over the bottom of one cookie and top with another cookie, right side up. Place on a small baking sheet in the freezer and repeat with the remaining cookies and ice cream.

2. Spread the chocolate chips on a plate. Roll each ice cream sandwich in the chips to coat the sides. Wrap the sandwiches individually in plastic wrap and freeze for 2 hours, or until firm, before serving.

S E R V E S   8

chocolate cookie
ice cream cake

COOLING OFF

NOTHING SAYS CHILDREN'S PARTY LIKE AN ice cream cake. You can tailor-make it with your little one's favorite ice cream. For the best results, start making this recipe early in the day, or even a few days ahead; it will keep in the freezer for several weeks. The ice cream should be well softened to make spreading easier, especially on the first layer. But freeze it after each layer is added to make it easier to add the next layer.

> 3 cups chocolate cookie crumbs
> 1 pint chocolate ice cream, softened
> 1 pint chocolate chip ice cream, softened
> 1 pint vanilla ice cream, softened
> 3/4 cup heavy cream
> 2 ounces white chocolate, chopped

1. Spread 1 cup of the cookie crumbs evenly in the bottom of a 9-inch springform pan. Spread the chocolate ice cream over the crumbs, smoothing with a metal spatula. Sprinkle another cup of the cookie crumbs evenly over the chocolate ice cream. Cover with plastic wrap and freeze for 1 hour.

2. Spread the chocolate chip ice cream in an even layer over the cookie crumbs, smoothing with a metal spatula. Sprinkle the remaining cup of cookie crumbs evenly over the chocolate chip ice cream. Cover with plastic wrap and freeze for 1 hour.

3. Spread the vanilla ice cream in an even layer over the cookie crumbs, smoothing with a metal spatula. Cover with plastic wrap and freeze for 4 hours, or until completely firm. Carefully remove the sides of the pan from the cake.

4. Meanwhile, in a double boiler over simmering, not boiling, water, combine 2 tablespoons of the heavy cream and the white chocolate. Heat the mixture, stirring, until the white chocolate is melted and smooth. Transfer the mixture to a bowl and let cool.

5. In a medium bowl, beat the remaining cream with an electric mixer until it thickens slightly. Add the white chocolate mixture and continue to beat until stiff peaks form. Spoon the whipped cream mixture into a pastry bag fitted with a large star tip and decorate the top of the ice cream cake.

6. Serve the cake immediately, or return it to the freezer, wrapped carefully in plastic, until ready to serve.

SERVES 8

chocolate–peanut butter
ice cream pie

MOUTHWATERING ICE-CREAM PIE WITH A crust made of crisped-rice cereal and melted chocolate—better than any crispy chocolate bar—this will not last long at a party!

CRISPY CHOCOLATE CRUST

1 (6-ounce) package semisweet chocolate chips

1/4 cup (1/2 stick) unsalted butter, cut in 4 pieces

1 1/2 cups crisped-rice cereal

2 pints peanut butter cup ice cream or
peanut butter ice cream, slightly softened
About 1 cup Dark Chocolate Sauce (p. 123)

1. Make the crispy chocolate crust. Line a 9-inch pie plate with foil. In the top of a double boiler over barely simmering water, melt the chocolate and butter, stirring occasionally until smooth. Remove from the heat, add the crisped-rice cereal, and stir until completely coated.

2. Transfer the mixture to the prepared pie plate and, using the back of a metal spoon, spread and press the mixture evenly over the the bottom and up the sides of the pan. Let cool, then cover and freeze for at least 1 hour, until hard.

3. Lift the chilled crust out of the pie plate, carefully peel off the foil, and return the crust to the pan. (This method ensures that the crust won't stick to the pan at serving time.) Spoon the ice cream into the crust and smooth the top. Cover and freeze for 1 hour, or until the ice cream is hard.

4. To serve, using a sharp heavy knife, cut the pie into wedges and place on serving plates. Drizzle about 2 tablespoons chocolate sauce over each serving.

SERVES 8

frozen *angel pie*

A N EDIBLE SERVING BOWL OF LIGHT, CRISP meringue is filled with luscious fruit sorbets and billowy whipped cream: This dessert looks like a cloud and tastes like heaven! You can make the meringue shell up to three days in advance. Store it in an airtight container to keep it fresh and crisp.

MERINGUE

3 large egg whites

3/4 cup granulated sugar

1/4 teaspoon cream of tartar

Pinch of salt

FILLING

1/2 cup heavy cream

1 tablespoon confectioners' sugar

1/2 pint mango sorbet

1/2 pint raspberry sorbet

1 kiwi, peeled and cut in lengthwise wedges

1. Make the meringue. Preheat the oven to 275°F. Line a baking sheet with waxed paper and grease the paper.

2. In a large bowl, beat the egg whites with an electric mixer until frothy. Increase the speed to medium-high and beat until the whites begin to form soft peaks. Add the granulated sugar, cream of tartar, and salt and continue to beat until the whites form stiff, glossy peaks.

3. Using a rubber spatula, spread some of the egg white mixture into a 9-inch circle on the prepared baking sheet. Build up the sides with more egg whites to form a bowl shape 2-inches high. Bake for 1 hour and 15 minutes, or until the shell is firm and dry, but not at all brown. Let cool completely on a wire rack.

4. Make the filling. In a medium bowl, beat the cream and confectioners' sugar with an electric mixer until stiff peaks form. Arrange scoops of sorbets into the meringue bowl in alternating colors. Decorate the top with dollops or rosettes of whipped cream and the kiwi wedges. Serve immediately.

SERVES 6

frozen
grasshopper pie

ERE A CHOCOLATE-SANDWICH COOKIE CRUST holds mint ice cream made extra mintier with crème de menthe. Although you could finish it simply with some chocolate shavings, for extra-special occasions, we suggest a topping of whipped cream rosettes, chocolate curls, and chocolate mints.

CHOCOLATE SANDWICH-COOKIE CRUMB CRUST

1 3/4 cups chocolate sandwich-cookie crumbs (from about 16 cookies)

3 tablespoons unsalted butter, melted and cooled

COOL MINT FILLING

2 pints mint chip ice cream, slightly softened

2 tablespoons crème de menthe

WHIPPED CREAM TOPPING

1/2 cup heavy cream

1 tablespoon sugar

3 or 4 chocolate-covered mints, halved, for garnish (optional)

Chocolate curls or shavings, for garnish (see Note)

Crème de menthe, for serving (optional)

1. Make the chocolate sandwich-cookie crumb crust. In a medium bowl, combine the cookie crumbs and butter and stir until the crumbs are evenly moistened. With your fingertips, press the mixture evenly over the bottom and up the side of a 9-inch pie plate. Cover and freeze for 1 hour, or until firm.

2. Make the cool mint filling. In a large bowl, combine the ice cream and crème de menthe, stirring until well blended. Spoon the ice cream mixture into the chilled crust and smooth the top. Freeze for 2 hours, or until the ice cream is hard.

3. Make the whipped cream topping. In a medium bowl, combine the cream and sugar and beat with an electric mixer until firm peaks form. Transfer the whipped cream to a pastry bag fitted with a large star tip and pipe 6 or 8 large rosettes around the edge of the pie. Stand a mint half in each rosette, if desired. Scatter the chocolate curls over the top of the ice cream.

4. To serve, using a sharp heavy knife, cut the pie into wedges and place on dessert plates. (If the crust sticks to the pan, dip the bottom of the pie plate briefly in very hot water to loosen.) Drizzle crème de menthe over each serving, if desired.

SERVES 6 TO 8

NOTE: To make chocolate curls or shavings, scrape a vegetable peeler across a block of room-temperature chocolate. (If necessary, warm the chocolate briefly under a lamp.)

deep dark *fudge sundaes*

OMEMADE FUDGE SAUCE, SPIKED WITH COFFEE liqueur, elevates these chocolatey sundaes to a bit of mocha heaven. The combination of the coffee-fudge sauce, chocolate ice cream and whipped cream is a classic for children of all ages although you could use any ice cream you wish.

**About 3/4 cup Best-Ever Hot Fudge Sauce
(p.124), warmed**

2 tablespoons coffee-flavored liqueur (optional)

1 cup heavy cream

2 tablespoons confectioners' sugar

1 quart chocolate ice cream

1/2 cup toasted slivered almonds (optional)

4 maraschino cherries, for garnish (optional)

1. In a small bowl, stir together the fudge sauce and the coffee liqueur, if desired.

2. In a medium bowl, beat the cream and confectioners' sugar with an electric mixer until stiff peaks form.

3. Spoon 1 tablespoon of the fudge sauce mixture into the bottom of 4 sundae glasses. Add 1 scoop of ice cream to each, then top with another tablespoon of fudge sauce. Repeat with 1 more scoop of ice cream and 1 tablespoon sauce in each glass.

4. Spoon the whipped cream on the sundaes. Garnish with the toasted almonds and cherries, if desired. Serve immediately.

SERVES 4

dark chocolate *sauce*

GREAT OVER ICE CREAM, OF COURSE, BUT this decadent dark sauce is also great drizzled around a slice of pound cake or a berry tartlet, or over peaches or poached pears.

> 5 ounces semisweet chocolate, finely chopped
>
> I cup heavy cream
>
> I/4 cup plus 2 tablespoons sugar
>
> I I/2 tablespoons unsalted butter, cut in 3 pieces
>
> I teaspoon vanilla extract

1. Place the chocolate in a medium bowl. In a small heavy saucepan, combine the cream, sugar, and butter. Bring just to a boil over medium-low heat, stirring to dissolve the sugar. Pour the cream mixture over the chocolate and let stand for 30 seconds, then whisk gently until the chocolate is melted and is smooth. Whisk in the vanilla.

2. Serve the sauce slightly warm or at room temperature. It can be made up to 5 days ahead, covered, and refrigerated. Reheat in a double boiler over barely simmering water, stirring occasionally.

MAKES ABOUT I 2/3 CUPS

creamy caramel *sauce*

STORE-BOUGHT CARAMEL SAUCE JUST DOESN'T compare with the homemade variety. This recipe proves it's a snap to make. Be sure to keep the children away from the stove; caramelized sugar is very hot.

> I cup sugar
>
> I/4 cup water
>
> 3/4 cup heavy cream

1. In a small deep heavy saucepan, combine the sugar and water and bring to a boil over medium-high heat, stirring to dissolve the sugar. Brush down the sides of the pan with a wet pastry brush to remove any sugar crystals. Boil, swirling the pan occasionally (not stirring), until the caramel is a golden amber color, 5 to 8 minutes.

2. Immediately remove the pan from the heat and, standing back to avoid splatters (the caramel will bubble up), add the cream. Stir with a wooden spoon, then set over low heat and cook, stirring, until completely smooth; be sure any hardened caramel on the bottom of the pan has dissolved.

3. Serve the sauce warm or at room temperature. It can be made up to 5 days ahead, covered, and refrigerated. Reheat over low heat, stirring occasionally.

MAKES ABOUT I I/4 CUPS

best-ever hot *fudge sauce*

W HEN YOU WANT A RICH, THICK, AND DELICIOUS sauce—good enough to eat by the spoonful—this is the one to make. The brown sugar lends a caramel undertone to the fudgy flavor.

1/2 cup heavy cream

1/2 cup packed light brown sugar

3 tablespoons granulated sugar

1/4 cup (1/2 stick) unsalted butter, cut in pieces

Pinch of salt

1/2 cup unsweetened cocoa powder, preferably
   Dutch-process

1/2 teaspoon vanilla extract

1. In a small heavy saucepan, combine the cream, brown and granulated sugars, butter, and salt and bring just to a simmer over medium heat, stirring to dissolve the sugar. Reduce the heat to medium-low and simmer for 2 minutes. Reduce the heat to low, add the cocoa, and whisk until smooth. Remove from the heat and stir in the vanilla.

2. Serve the sauce hot or warm. It can be made up to 5 days ahead and refrigerated. Reheat in a double boiler over simmering water, stirring occasionally.

MAKES ABOUT 1 1/4 CUPS

raspberry *sauce*

U SE THIS VIBRANT SAUCE AS A TOPPING FOR ice cream or pound cake. Because it freezes well for up to six months, it's a good way to preserve berries at the height of the season for a taste of summer in the cold winter months.

1/2 cup sugar

1/3 cup water

2 cups fresh, or thawed frozen, raspberries

1 tablespoon fresh lemon juice or Chambord
   (black raspberry liqueur)

1. In a small saucepan, bring the sugar and water to a boil over medium high heat. Stir the mixture until the sugar dissolves, about 5 minutes. Add the raspberries and cook for 2 minutes, stirring.

2. Transfer the mixture to a food processor or blender and process until pureed.

3. Pour the raspberry sauce through a strainer set over a medium bowl, pressing on the solids with the back of a wooden spoon to extract all the liquid; discard the solids. Stir in the lemon juice. Let the sauce cool completely before using. It will keep for 3 days in the refrigerator or freeze for longer storage.

MAKES ABOUT 2 CUPS

COOLING OFF

Chapter Seven
cookies & candies

the ultimate chocolate brownies

USING BOTH COCOA POWDER AND UNSWEETENED chocolate makes these brownies extra rich and extremely dense. Just one bite and you'll agree that they're the very best! When melting chocolate with butter, always put the butter in the pan first to avoid overheating the chocolate.

I cup (2 sticks) unsalted butter

4 ounces unsweetened chocolate, coarsely chopped

2 cups sugar

4 large eggs

I teaspoon vanilla extract

1/2 cup all-purpose flour

1/4 cup unsweetened cocoa powder

2/3 cup coarsely chopped walnuts

1. Preheat the oven to 350°F. Grease a 12- x 9-inch baking pan. Set aside.

2. In a medium saucepan, melt the butter and chocolate over low heat. Remove from the heat and let cool for about 10 minutes.

3. In a medium bowl, beat the sugar and eggs with an electric mixer for 5 to 6 minutes, until thick and lemon colored. Beat in the vanilla.

4. Using a large rubber spatula, gently fold the chocolate mixture into the egg mixture until thoroughly mixed.

5. Sift together the flour and cocoa and fold gently into the batter, mixing until just blended. Fold in the walnuts. Pour the batter into the prepared pan.

6. Bake the brownies for 25 to 30 minutes, until the center is just set and a toothpick inserted in the center comes out with just a few crumbs. Do not overbake. Let the brownies cool on a wire rack for 30 minutes. Using a small sharp knife, cut into 24 bars.

MAKES 2 DOZEN BARS

QUEEN OF THE KITCHEN TIP

Additions to Brownies

Brownies are a wonderful base for other ingredients and you could add any of the following to customize your cookies:

At the very end of the recipe, before you pour the batter into the pan, add 1/4 cup of any of the following: mini chocolate chips, white chips, butterscotch chips, coconut, crispy M&M's, Reese's Pieces, chopped toffee bars, or chopped caramels.

coconut–krispie *treats*

eVERYONE'S FAVORITE MARSHMALLOW TREATS get a tropical makeover with coconut and banana in these easy, no-bake bars. We've flavored them with coconut but, if you like, try some other additions such as small chocolate candies, small peanut butter-flavored candies, or mini chocolate chips.

> 1 (10-ounce) package marshmallows
>
> 3 tablespoons unsalted butter
>
> 6 cups crisped-rice cereal
>
> 1 cup unsweetened shredded coconut
>
> 1 banana, mashed

1. Grease a 13- x 9- inch baking pan.

2. In a large microwave-proof bowl, combine the marshmallows and butter and microwave on medium power for 2 minutes. Stir and microwave for 1 minute more.

3. Add the crisped-rice cereal, coconut, and banana and stir to combine.

4. Transfer the mixture to the prepared pan and press down with a rubber spatula. Let cool completely on a wire rack. Using a large sharp knife, cut into 24 squares. Store in a single layer in an airtight container.

MAKES 2 DOZEN BARS

QUEEN OF THE KITCHEN TIP

Packing Cookies to Give as Gifts

Cookies make the perfect gift from your kitchen, especially at holiday time. Just be sure to pack them carefully so there's no danger of breakage (or crumbling). An assortment of cookies is always nice, but keep in mind that hard and soft cookies shouldn't be stored together for any length of time, or the crisper cookies will soften. Colorful tins are attractive and practical containers, but be creative: Small baskets and inexpensive painted boxes are lovely too. Use brightly colored tissue paper to line your cookie container to make it look even more festive. Depending on the cookies you are giving, you may want to layer them carefully between double layers of waxed paper, or just arrange them in an attractive jumble. Brownies and other bar cookies can be wrapped individually in colored plastic wrap. And if you're really concerned about breakage, plain popped popcorn (the real kind, not the styrofoam packing type) can be scattered over and around the cookies for added protection.

coffee toffee bars

COFFEE AND TOFFEE ARE A CLASSIC AMERICAN combination that is brought together in these rich, buttery bars.

2 teaspoons instant coffee granules

1 teaspoon vanilla extract

1 cup (2 sticks) unsalted butter,
   at room temperature

1 1/3 cups packed light brown sugar

2 large eggs, at room temperature

1/4 teaspoon salt

1 3/4 cups all-purpose flour

4 (1.4-ounce) milk chocolate-covered crisp
   butter toffee bars, coarsely chopped

1. Preheat the oven to 350°F. Grease a 9- x 13-inch baking pan.

2. In a small cup, dissolve the coffee granules in the vanilla. Set aside.

3. In a large bowl, beat the butter and brown sugar with an electric mixer until light and fluffy. Add the eggs one at a time, beating well after each addition. Stir in the salt. Scrape down the sides of the bowl and beat in the coffee mixture. On low speed, beat in the flour in 2 additions. With a wooden spoon, stir in the chopped candy bars. Pour the batter into the prepared pan and smooth the top.

4. Bake the bars for 22 to 25 minutes, until a toothpick inserted into the center comes out clean. Let cool completely on a wire rack. Using a large heavy sharp knife, cut into 24 bars.

MAKES 2 DOZEN BARS

chewy chocolate *coconut bars*

fOR COCONUT LOVERS, THESE BARS ARE irresistible. The coconut not only gives the cookies a wonderful, almost nutty flavor, but also lends a great deal of moisture which makes them so chewy.

> 10 tablespoons (1 1/4 sticks) unsalted butter
> 1 2/3 cups shortbread cookie crumbs
>   (about 24 cookies)
> 1 3/4 cups sweetened flaked coconut
> 2 (3-ounce) bars bittersweet chocolate,
>   coarsely chopped
> 1 (14-ounce) can sweetened condensed milk

1. Preheat the oven to 350°F.

2. Melt the butter in a small saucepan. Pour it into a 9- x 13-inch baking pan, tilting the pan so the butter covers the bottom evenly. Sprinkle the cookie crumbs evenly over the bottom of the pan. Sprinkle 3/4 cup coconut evenly over the crumbs. Scatter the chocolate over the coconut, then scatter the remaining coconut over the chocolate. Drizzle the condensed milk evenly over the top.

3. Bake the bars for 22 to 25 minutes, until the coconut is golden brown in spots and the condensed milk is bubbling. Let the bars cool completely on a wire rack. Refrigerate briefly for easier cutting. Using a large sharp knife, cut into 30 bars. Serve at room temperature or chilled.

MAKES 2 1/2 DOZEN BARS

triple chocolate *chip chippers*

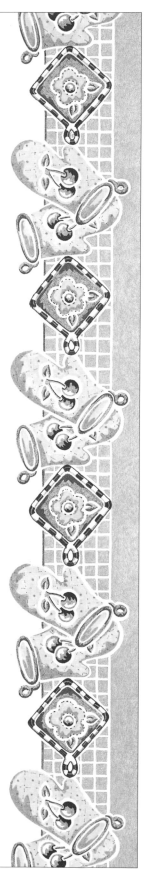

fILLED WITH WHITE AND MILK CHOCOLATE chips, chunks of bittersweet chocolate, and, instead of the more traditional walnuts, buttery pecans, these wonderful afternoon treats pack a wollop. They have a little of everything for everyone!

2 1/3 cups all-purpose flour

1 teaspoon baking soda

3/4 teaspoon salt

1 cup (2 sticks) unsalted butter, at room
   temperature

1 cup packed light brown sugar

2/3 cup granulated sugar

2 large eggs

2 teaspoons vanilla extract

2 (3-ounce) bars bittersweet chocolate,
   cut in 1/4 to 1/2-inch pieces

2/3 cup white chocolate chips

2/3 cup milk chocolate chips

3/4 cup pecans, coarsely chopped

1. Preheat the oven to 350°F. Lightly grease two baking sheets.

2. In a medium bowl, whisk together the flour, baking soda, and salt. Set aside.

3. In a large bowl, beat the butter and brown and granulated sugars with an electric mixer until light and fluffy. Add the eggs one at a time, beating well after each addition. Beat in the vanilla.

4. On low speed, gradually add the flour mixture in two additions. Using a large wooden spoon, stir in the bittersweet chocolate, the white and chocolate chips, and the pecans.

5. Drop the dough by slightly rounded tablespoonfuls about 2 inches apart onto the prepared baking sheets.

6. Bake the cookies for 9 to 11 minutes, until the edges are golden brown. Let cool for 2 to 3 minutes on the baking sheets, then transfer the cookies to wire racks to cool completely.

MAKES ABOUT 5 DOZEN COOKIES

coconut *macaroons*

tHESE TRADITIONAL SWEET TREATS ARE EASY to whip up. Just don't try to make them on a humid day, or they will be too soft. Be sure to let the macaroons cool completely before removing them from the foil; they need time to firm up.

3 large egg whites

Pinch of salt

1 cup sugar

1 teaspoon vanilla extract

1 (7-ounce) bag sweetened shredded coconut

1. Preheat the oven to 325°F. Line two large baking sheets with foil and grease the foil.

2. In a large bowl, beat the egg whites with an electric mixer until frothy. Add the salt, increase the speed to medium-high, and beat until the whites begin to form soft peaks. Beat in the sugar about 1 tablespoon at a time and continue beating until stiff peaks form.

3. Beat in the vanilla. Using a large rubber spatula, fold in the coconut.

4. Drop the batter by heaping teaspoonfuls about 1 1/2 inches apart onto the prepared baking sheets.

5. Bake the macaroons for 15 to 18 minutes, until they are light golden and just set. Let the baking sheets cool completely on wire racks.

6. Carefully peel the macaroons off the foil and store in an airtight container.

MAKES ABOUT 5 DOZEN MACAROONS

QUEEN OF THE KITCHEN TIP

Macaroons

Macaroons are a classic French and Italian sweet, with dozens of different regional versions and variations. Almond macaroons, made with almond paste, are probably the most traditional, but coconut macaroons are another great favorite. Homemade macaroons are a wonderful quick treat and far more delicious than store-bought. And macaroons can be dressed up in endless ways, according to your own personal taste by adding all sorts of "mix-ins" to the batter. After you've added the coconut, you can fold in up to a cup of mini chocolate chips, coarsely chopped nuts, chopped candied orange peel, even chopped candied cherries, whatever takes your fancy. Or make your macaroons really elegant by dipping each baked and cooled cookie into melted chocolate, coating it halfway.

COOKIES & CANDIES

candy cane butter cookies

OUR CRUNCHY CANDY CANE COOKIES ARE A twist on traditional Christmas butter cookies and will be in demand long after the holidays have passed. You can vary the recipe using other crushed hard candies, such as butterscotch or lemon, but then you should omit the peppermint extract.

1 cup (2 sticks) unsalted butter, at room temperature

3/4 cup sugar

2 large egg yolks

1/4 teaspoon peppermint extract

1/4 teaspoon salt

2 1/4 cups all-purpose flour

1 egg white

1 cup crushed candy canes

1. In a large bowl, beat the butter and sugar with an electric mixer until light and fluffy. Add the egg yolks, peppermint extract, and salt and beat until combined. On low speed, gradually beat in the flour.

2. Divide the dough into thirds, shape each piece into a disk, and wrap in plastic. Refrigerate for at least 2 hours, or until ready to use.

3. Preheat the oven to 350°F.

4. On a lightly floured surface, roll out 1 disk of the dough to 3/16 inch thick. Cut out shapes with 2-inch cookie cutters and place 2 inches apart on ungreased baking sheets. Repeat with the remaining dough.

5. Beat the egg white until frothy. Brush over the cookies and sprinkle with the crushed candy canes.

6. Bake the cookies for 15 to 17 minutes, until the edges just begin to brown. Let the cookies cool for 5 minutes on the baking sheets, then transfer to wire racks and cool completely.

MAKES ABOUT 3 DOZEN COOKIES

jumbo peanut *butter cookies*

1 ET THE KIDS HELP SHAPE THESE FAVORITE after-school cookies; they love to make the traditional crisscross design on top. We like the crunch of the peanuts, but if you're a fan of smooth peanut butter you can use it instead.

3 cups all-purpose flour

1 teaspoon baking soda

1/4 teaspoon salt

1 cup (2 sticks) unsalted butter,
at room temperature

1 1/2 cups granulated sugar

3/4 cup packed light brown sugar

1 cup chunky peanut butter

2 large eggs

1 1/2 teaspoons vanilla extract

1. Preheat the oven to 350°F. Lightly grease two baking sheets.

2. In a medium bowl, whisk together the flour, baking soda, and salt.

3. In a large bowl, preferably the bowl of a standing electric mixer, beat the butter and the granulated and brown sugars with an electric mixer until light and fluffy. Beat in the peanut butter. Add the eggs one at a time, beating well after each addition. Beat in the vanilla. On low speed, beat in the flour mixture in two additions.

4. Shape rounded tablespoonfuls of the dough into balls and place 2 inches apart on the prepared baking sheets. With a fork, make a crisscross pattern on the top of each cookie, flattening it into a 2 1/4-inch round.

5. Bake for 11 to 13 minutes, until the edges of the cookies are light golden brown but the centers are still soft. Let cool for 1 to 2 minutes on the baking sheets, then transfer to wire racks to cool completely.

MAKES ABOUT 4 DOZEN COOKIES

five-minute *fudge*

HIS RICH DEEP-CHOCOLATE FUDGE IS MUCH simpler and quicker to make than the classic, and it comes out smooth and creamy every time. We recommend a good-quality bittersweet or semisweet chocolate, but to make the recipe even easier, you can substitute 2 2/3 cups semisweet chocolate chips for the chopped chocolate.

> 1 pound bittersweet or semisweet chocolate, coarsely chopped
> 1 (14-ounce) can sweetened condensed milk
> Pinch of salt
> 1 cup chopped walnuts (optional)
> 2 teaspoons vanilla extract

1. Line an 8-inch square baking pan with foil, leaving a 1-inch foil overhang over two opposite sides of the pan. In the top of a large double boiler over very gently simmering water, melt the chocolate with the condensed milk and salt, stirring until smooth.

2. Remove the pan from the heat and stir in the walnuts, if using, and the vanilla. Pour the fudge into the prepared pan and using a rubber spatula, smooth the top. Let cool, then refrigerate for 2 hours, or until set.

3. Using the foil overhang as handles, lift the fudge out of the pan. Peel off the foil and, using a heavy sharp knife, cut the fudge into 36 squares.

MAKES 3 DOZEN SQUARES

QUEEN OF THE KITCHEN TIP

Melting Chocolate

As rich and delicious as it is, chocolate can be temperamental to work with and difficult to melt. It burns very easily, so be very careful not to overheat it. The best way to melt it is either in a double boiler over (not in) barely simmering, not boiling, water or in a microwave at medium or low power. If using a microwave, stir the chocolate at frequent intervals to check its consistency, it may still hold its shape when it's actually melted. White chocolate and milk chocolate are even more prone to burning than dark chocolates, so take extra care with them.

When you are melting chocolate by itself, just a drop of water can cause it to "seize," becoming gritty, lumpy, and unworkable. Make sure the pan or bowl you are using is thoroughly dry before you put the chocolate in, be careful not to let any moisture drip onto the chocolate, and, if using a double boiler, once the chocolate is melted, quickly lift the pan of chocolate up and away from the steaming water below it.

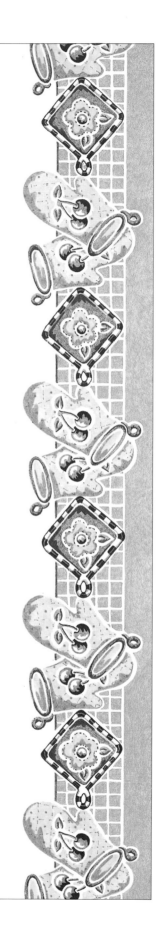

chocolate cognac *truffles*

FOR SOMETHING SO SIMPLE TO MAKE, THESE chocolate truffles are a remarkably sophisticated after-dinner treat. Be sure to make them several hours (or a few days) in advance, so they have time to set. If you do not like cognac, simply omit it from the recipe.

> 1 1/2 cups heavy cream
> 12 ounces bittersweet chocolate, finely chopped
> 2 teaspoons cognac (optional)
> 1/3 cup unsweetened cocoa powder

1. In a small saucepan, heat the cream over high heat until it comes to a simmer.

2. Meanwhile, place the chocolate in a medium bowl. Pour the scalded cream into the bowl and let sit for 2 minutes. Stir until the chocolate has melted and the mixture is smooth. Stir in the cognac, if desired.

3. Pour the truffle mixture into a bowl and let cool completely. Cover the dish with plastic wrap and refrigerate until set, about 4 hours.

4. Pour the cocoa into a shallow dish or plate and set aside. Using a melon baller or teaspoon, scoop the truffle mixture in 1-inch balls. Roll the balls in the cocoa to coat evenly.

MAKES ABOUT 3 DOZEN TRUFFLES

chocolate-dipped *strawberries*

YOU CAN USE ANY GOOD CHOCOLATE TO COAT the fruit in this recipe, or a combination for a decorative effect. When buying strawberries, keep your eye on the color: you want the tops to be red since that is the end visible after dipping. If you can find strawberries with stems, they make a very attractive presentation and provide the perfect handle for these luscious delicacies.

3 ounces bittersweet, semisweet, or white chocolate,
    coarsely chopped
Scant 1 tablespoon vegetable shortening
1 pint medium to large strawberries,
    patted thoroughly dry

1. In a double boiler over very gently simmering water, melt the chocolate with the vegetable shortening, stirring until smooth. Remove from the heat.

2. Line a work surface with waxed paper. Dip each strawberry into the chocolate, turning to coat almost completely with the chocolate and letting the excess drip off. Carefully place on the waxed paper. Tilt the pan as necessary to make coating easier; if the chocolate begins to set, return the pan briefly to the heat to remelt it.

3. Let the berries stand until the chocolate is set, about 30 minutes, then carefully remove them from the waxed paper. Serve, or refrigerate for up to 8 hours.

SERVES 4 TO 6

chocolate-dipped *apricots*

USE THE LARGEST, PLUMPEST DRIED APRICOTS to make these delicious treats. Dried pears and dried pineapple would also work well.

3 ounces bittersweet, semisweet, or white chocolate,
    coarsely chopped
Scant 1 tablespoon vegetable shortening
4 ounces dried apricots

1. In a double boiler over very gently simmering water, melt the chocolate with the vegetable shortening, stirring until smooth. Remove from the heat.

2. Line a work surface with waxed paper. Holding one end of each apricot, dip it halfway into the chocolate, turning to coat on both sides and letting the excess drip off. Carefully place on the waxed paper. Tilt the pan as necessary to make coating easier; if the chocolate begins to set, return the pan briefly to the heat to remelt it.

3. Let the apricots stand until the chocolate is set, about 30 minutes, then carefully remove them from the waxed paper, peeling it away from the chocolate. Serve, or store in an airtight container at room temperature for up to 5 days.

SERVES 4 TO 6

chocolate macadamia *buttercrunch*

S UBSTITUTING RICH, BUTTERY MACADAMIA nuts for almonds makes this variation of the classic toffee candy even better than the original. Serve this on its own with coffee or crush it over ice cream.

1 1/3 cups sugar

1 cup (2 sticks) unsalted butter, cut in pieces

2 tablespoons light corn syrup

2 tablespoons water

2 (3.25-ounce) jars macadamia nuts, coarsely chopped

1 teaspoon vanilla extract

6 ounces semisweet chocolate, coarsely chopped

1. Line a 10- x 15-inch baking sheet with foil and lightly grease the foil.

2. In a large deep heavy saucepan, combine the sugar, butter, corn syrup, and water and cook over medium heat, stirring with a wooden spoon, for about 5 minutes, until the butter has melted and the sugar is dissolved. Brush down the sides of the pan with a wet pastry brush to remove any sugar crystals. Bring to a boil; brush down the sides of the pan again. Boil, stirring frequently with a clean wooden spoon, until the toffee reaches 300°F (hard crack stage, see tip at right) on a candy thermometer.

3. Immediately remove the pan from the heat and stir in half the nuts and the vanilla. Working quickly (be careful, the toffee will be very hot), pour the toffee onto the prepared baking sheet and tilt the sheet to spread it evenly (the baking sheet will become very hot). Let cool completely.

4. In a double boiler set over very gently simmering water, melt the chocolate, stirring occasionally until smooth. Pour the chocolate onto the toffee and spread it evenly with a rubber spatula. Sprinkle the remaining nuts over the top. Let cool until the chocolate has set, then break the toffee into pieces.

MAKES ABOUT 1 1/2 POUNDS

QUEEN OF THE KITCHEN TIP

Working with Sugar

Melted sugar and caramel can be dangerously hot (caramel can reach a temperature of 350°F—a lot hotter than boiling water). Keep the kids away from the stove, and be sure to use a heavy pot, with the handle turned toward the back of the stove. The temperature of cooked sugar can be tested either with a candy thermometer or by dropping a bit of the syrup from the tip of a spoon into a glass of cold water and determining the stage it has reached this way (sugar stages range from "thread," about 230°F, up to "hard crack," about 300°F; caramel, which is even hotter, is usually judged by color, from light to dark amber, rather than by temperature.)

COOKIES & CANDIES

almond *brittle*

aLMOND BRITTLE IS THE GROWN-UP VERSION of peanut brittle. Make this a day ahead and let the flavors mature and mellow overnight. This would be great as part of a holiday assortment of cookies and candy.

2 cups sugar

1/8 teaspoon cream of tartar

1/3 cup water

1 tablespoon unsalted butter, cut in 4 pieces

1 cup whole unblanched almonds, toasted

1. Lightly oil a baking sheet. Oil the back of a wooden spoon. Set aside.

2. In a large deep heavy saucepan, combine the sugar, cream of tartar, and water and bring to a boil over medium-high heat, stirring to dissolve the sugar. Brush down the sides of the pan with a wet pastry brush to remove any sugar crystals. Boil, without stirring, 8 to 10 minutes, until the caramel is a golden amber color (swirl the caramel in the pan occasionally for even cooking).

3. Immediately remove the pan from the heat and add the butter and nuts. Stir carefully with a wooden spoon just until the almonds are coated with caramel. Working quickly, pour the caramel onto the prepared baking sheet and, using the oiled wooden spoon, spread the brittle out on the sheet, separating any clusters of almonds (the pan will become very hot). Let cool completely.

4. Break the cooled brittle into pieces. Serve, or store in an airtight container at room temperature for up to 2 weeks.

MAKES ABOUT 1 1/4 POUNDS

index